Empowered By The *Dream:*

A Journey of Resilience

Gladys A. Barrio

Empowered by the Dream - Reviews

"Empowered by the Dream: A Journey of Resilience is a beautiful story of one family's journey of survival. Through the tale of her family, Gladys A. Barrio brings to us the tales of millions of exiles who had to go through the travails of the Spanish Civil War and suffer under Fidel Castro's communist regime in Cuba. The book is a heart-touching tale that sheds light on the plight of immigrants and exiles. I loved Gladys A. Barrio's book. This book is highly recommended to fans of biographies and creative nonfiction books. People who have an interest in Cuba will love this book. Gladys A. Barrio is a brilliant author. She has drawn from the stories told by her parents, aunts, uncles, and friends as well as her own experiences to craft this masterpiece. Her writing is vivid and heartfelt. It made me feel I was there."

Kajori Sheryl Paul » 07 May 2024
OnlineBookClub.org ★★★★★

"One of the most compelling aspects of the novel is its exploration of the immigrant experience and the search for belonging in a new land. As the Barrio Castañer family navigates the challenges of starting anew in the New World, they encounter discrimination, poverty, and cultural barriers. Yet, amidst the hardships, they also find moments of joy, friendship, and resilience, highlighting the resilience and adaptability of the human spirit."

Diana Rodriguez » March 26, 2024
Goodreads ★★★★★

"What emerges from these interconnected narratives is a powerful exploration of the cyclical nature of history and the enduring human quest for belonging and prosperity. Despite the passage of time and the changing tides of fortune, the challenges faced by each generation of the family echo with haunting familiarity, underscoring the resilience and strength that have been passed down through the ages."

Joshua Ferguson » March 27, 2024
Goodreads ★★★★★

"I just finished reading "Empowered by the Dream," and I'm still reeling from the emotional journey it took me on. This stunning book masterfully weaves together the stories of three generations of the Barrio Castañer family as they navigate exile, emigration, war, poverty, and love. From the opening pages set in Havana, Cuba, I was hooked. The author skillfully transported me to Spain, jumping between different time periods, as the family's ancestors sought a better life, only to face repeating cycles of political upheaval, war, and exile. Through the characters' struggles and triumphs, I felt a deep connection to their resilience and determination. The stories of Alfredo and Enedina, and their ancestors, are a testament to the power of hope and the human spirit. The full-color format added a vibrant layer of depth to the narrative, making the characters and settings come alive in a way that felt almost cinematic.

Overall, "Empowered by the Dream" is a sweeping and powerful tale of family, love, and perseverance. I highly recommend it to anyone looking for a compelling and emotionally resonant read."

Tailleen Arias Corujo » April 3, 2024
Philanthropist and Entrepreneur - Amazon 

"When your dream, once nothing more than a seed, blossoms into full bloom, you inspire the world to cultivate their own gardens. Gladys Barrio, a chemist and chemistry professor had a dream. She longed to document her family's journey from Cuba and tell their story. Many immigrants share this desire, as their stories are often powerful illustrations of overcoming obstacles, becoming resilient, and the power of never losing hope."

Carolyn De Posada » April 4, 2024
Author of "Looking Over the Edge", Attorney At Law, Motivational Speaker, and Life Coach - Instagram Post 

"The book is a wonderful and compelling read that pulled me right in and kept me wanting to learn more. The author powerfully shows the theme of resilience. She has a noteworthy talent for painting appealing and interesting characters, dialogue, and situations. As someone who was raised in the U.S., the book both taught and entertained me about the challenges and difficulties of war, political turmoil, and escape, as well as perseverance, human connection, and love. BRAVO!!!!"

Scott Scovel » March 25, 2024
Writer and Entrepreneur ★★★★★

"A wonderfully written book that takes you on a very emotional journey. The book opened my eyes to the difficulties of emigration from Cuba and how this family overcame all the obstacles because of the future life that they saw for themselves and because of their love for each other. It interweaves history with family saga. I recommend it highly."

Regine Rayevsky Fisher » April 10, 2024
Author of "Dance Me To The End Of Love" ★★★★★

"Gladys Barrio had a dream...to write a book about her ancestors and how they were able to emigrate from Spain to Cuba during the Spanish Civil War, looking for the freedom they did not have in their home country. In a vivid style she relates the struggles the family endured in order to achieve their dreams. Along the way they encountered many obstacles but in the end they triumphed. Glady's scholarly background is manifested in her writing style which uses history as a backdrop to set the scene for the events taking place around her characters. The author made her dream come true and so did her family! An easy-to-read, very enjoyable book."

Lomberto Perez-Placencia » May 5, 2024
Author of "The Parker Pen Incident" 

*"It was the best of times. It was the worst of times,
it was the age of wisdom, it was the age of foolishness,
it was the epoch of belief, it was the epoch of incredulity,
it was the season of light, it was the season of darkness,
it was the spring of hope, it was the winter of despair."*

Charles Dickens

DEDICATION

To my dear parents and ancestors.
My amazing daughters, Jenny and Jackie.
My Adored Grandchildren: Emily, Sophia, Samantha,
Lucas, and Sarah.
And Jesus, my fiancé and inspiration.

"May the exemplary resiliency of our ancestors be a guiding light leading the way in the midst of darkness."

G.A. Barrio

IN HONOR OF THE ADVOCATES OF FREEDOM

This book is written to honor all those who spent their lives fighting to survive exile while dreaming of the return to their homeland, for all those who contributed to the cause of freedom, who every day anguished over the suffering of their compatriots still living in tyranny, and who daily feverishly prayed for the freedom of their country.

But it's primarily dedicated to those who die in exile, never fulfilling the dream of returning to their adored native land.

Dad, this book is in your honor. May your soul now soar with the freedom you fervently craved on your beloved island, the land unjustly torn from your grasp. May the wings of your spirit carry you to every corner of cherished Santiago de Cuba, where your fondest childhood memories reside.

Like the tempest's wind, may your soul swiftly journey back to Havana, reclaiming its rightful place once more. May you see the city that you loved but barely had a chance to get to know since all your time was dedicated to hard work and creating the future that you never saw. The future that those people so heartlessly took from you. But may you see not the destroyed country that it is now, rather the Cuba that could have been, the Cuba that you dreamed of but never was. Maybe, just maybe, one far away day, it will be free again thanks to people like you who never stopped fighting for the dream. Thank you for all you did for us, for your country, for your family, for your friends, and even for those you knew and helped but who could not even call friends. Many may not remember.

Some will say, "Oh! Abuelo, bisabuelo, that man! For what we now are and what future generations will be, thank you for your exemplary life. Thank you for your dreams."

CONTENTS

1

FEAR

THIS WILL NOT LAST MORE THAN A YEAR
Havana, Cuba.
1960-1961

Alfredo[1] whispered in anguish as he phoned Roberto, *"Cuñado* - brother-in-law, you were right! This man is nothing but a vile communist who lied and betrayed each one of us and his country."

There was excruciating pain in Alfredo Barrio's eyes, realizing that the revolution he had so strongly supported was not what it claimed to be. The leader who so many people placed their hopes on was a cruel, bloody dictator whose only goal was to gain power for himself at the price of destroying the island they so loved.

September 1960 marked a ghastly year for Cuban families. Innocent people, anyone suspected of not supporting the revolution, were executed by firing squads at *Paredones de Fusilamiento* – execution walls. Some sources suggest that as many as 49,000 individuals were shot by firing squads in Cuba after 1959.[2] Others were unjustly thrown into jail, tortured, and left to rot and die in confined, dirty cells.[3] Fear overcame every corner of the nation. Out on the streets and even inside homes, whispering for fear of incarceration had become the norm. Businesses were confiscated by the government and those who owned them were left on the streets.[4]

"*Mi hermano* - my brother, I'd warned you, but you did not want to believe," responded Roberto, exhaling pain from his lungs. "Remember your dad always used to say, '*Es mejor un malo conocido que un bueno por conocer* - Better the devil you know than the devil you don't.' How right he was."

"How could I fathom this would happen when we did so much for this son-of-a-bitch!" Alfredo exclaimed, nervously rubbing his head with his hands. "How could anyone predict this outcome? How could anyone be so evil to pull a betrayal like this on his own people?"

"*Cuñado*, I'm seeing what's happening on the streets every day. Remember, I'm the one who is sent to record the evils of this new government. Do you think that I like doing this? I hate it! First, I had to do it for Batista, and now for this false revolution, which is a hundredfold more severe. This regime is killing far more innocent people than the previous dictatorship."

Roberto was a fiscal attorney whose job was to witness and record the removal of the deceased, as well as the seized properties. Out in the field, he had seen the true colors of the revolution from its inception.

Over the last few months, the brothers-in-law, like many others throughout the island, had many verbal altercations about the outcome of the political transformation of the island. Alfredo could not believe that the revolution that he and many others had so strongly supported was nothing but a betrayal that would bring death and destruction to his country.

He felt regret at the memory of the time when he walked on his knees toward the Lady of Charity Shrine, praying for the success of the revolution.

How wrong was I. He thought.

"*Cuñado*, what are we going to do? Enedina is panicking, recalling her ordeal during the Spanish Civil War after her parents returned to their homeland. She is so scared for our girls, but if we leave the country, we lose everything we have worked so hard for. What are we to do?" whispered Alfredo, in fear someone would overhear the call.

"I don't know what to do, myself. What I know is that we need to save our kids." He stopped briefly, "But now we must cut this conversation short because they may be tapping our phones. I will call you soon."

Enedina, Alfredo's wife of Spanish descent but born in Cuba, had lived through the bloody Spanish Civil War of the 1930s. She recalled the terror she experienced as an 11-year-old, fleeing in the middle of the night with her parents, two older brothers, and sister.

"Alfredo, we cannot forget what happened in Spain during the war." Enedina reminded her husband, "The same may happen here." She paused, then said, "Entire classes of children were taken from schools by the Red Cross into other countries to save them from the horrors of the war—many never saw their parents again."[5]

"I know, Eni," as she was endearingly called, "the children who were taken to Russia were indoctrinated into the Marxist–Leninist philosophy and never returned home. Some came back on their own as adults. However, the ones taken to other countries were sent back after the war." Alfredo put his hand on his wife's shoulder.

"I'm so scared. I don't think I could handle a similar fate for my daughters. We must do something now!" She implored in a panic.

In September of 1960, one year after Castro took over Cuba and General Fulgencio Batista fled the country, Alfredo, and Enedina, like many other Cuban families, decided to take the risk of flying their daughters to an unfamiliar country.

One muggy and dreadful morning, Alfredo and Enedina prepared their two young daughters, Mary, and Gladys, to leave the island.

"Is it two or three changes of clothing that they are allowed to take?" Enedina asked nervously, packing the kids' luggage. "How can they survive with so little clothing? They are kids who need to change often."

"Don't worry so much about that. I think they'll get uniforms at the school," Alfredo continued. Then he whispered, "What's important is to cover the hidden compartment I built inside the single suitcase they are taking to smuggle the $100 bill they may need."

The luggage preparation was detailed because of the recent restrictions imposed by the Castro regime. Alfredo was to travel with his two daughters to Kingston, Jamaica, where he had already enrolled them in a Catholic boarding school. Subsequently, uncertain about the political state of the island, he planned to return to Cuba to secure his business and home. The proximity of the islands and the idea that their return would be imminent made Kingston seem a convenient place.

"They will be back soon. This will not last more than a year!" said Alfredo, echoing the same belief of the ever-increasing august number of opponents to the revolution, given the atrocities and injustices impacting every family.

A palpable restlessness consumed Alfredo and Enedina that evening as he and the girls prepared to embark on a journey filled with uncertainties.

Although the dream lives their young family had painstakingly woven were now crumbling in front of their eyes, they sought refuge in the fortitude of their ancestors as they talked about the ordeals their parents endured to reach Cuba, the promised land of opportunities.

For Alfredo, the hardships were softened over time since the Barrio family began to arrive in Cuba early at the turn of the century. Not so for Enedina Castañer, whose memories of war were sharpened by the situation on the island.

They held each other, hanging on to the recollection of their ancestors' resilience, hoping it would guide them through the darkness of the present time.

2

BAUTISTA AND MARIA[6]
*From Teruel, Aragon, Spain
to Oriente, Cuba.
1916 to 1931*

Enedina remembered being told that decades earlier, in the Aragon region of Spain, a young man named Mateo coaxed her father, Bautista, to attend a funeral.

"Bautista, please, come with me to Aguaviva. I have a funeral to attend, and I don't want to travel by myself. Come with me."

Both friends lived in Mas de las Matas, a municipality of the province of Teruel, Aragon, Spain, located between the valley of the Ebro River and the foothills of the Iberian Mountain range. It was 1919, and twenty-six-year-old Bautista was a man working hard to fulfill the bright future that he envisioned for himself.

"Why would I want to attend a funeral?" responded Bautista.

"Come on, it's only four kilometers away, and I hear that there are many beautiful girls in Aguaviva."

The thought of attractive young women immediately appealed to Bautista. Aguaviva was considered the gateway to the Lower Aragon region from the neighboring province of Castellón. The small town located in the Mas de las Matas Basin is crossed by the rivers Guadalupe and Bergantes, the waters of which are the origin of the town's name.

Bautista was persuaded to accompany Mateo on this short trip, which would transform his life forever. As they arrived in Aguaviva, they entered a ragged, poor village shack where the funeral was beginning. They gently forced their way through the crowd, which felt like a tunnel of darkness impregnated by the pungent smell of agglomerated zombies, the attendees' heads covered, dressed in old, dark, heavy garments and rags. Rancid fumes invaded the shack. They encountered people of all ages with big teary eyes, each one moving back slowly, allowing the newcomers, in snail-like motion, to eventually reach the coffin.

Two beautiful, grieving young ladies, daughters of the deceased, were standing next to the coffin. They wore black tunics, dark heavy khimars, and had swollen red faces from long hours of weeping and sobbing. Laments were heard throughout the gloomy room.

Bautista's eyes were immediately drawn to the youngest of the two daughters, Maria. However, being the respectful young man he was, he controlled his eyes, disguising his attraction.

That evening, as the rays of the sun vanished from the earth and the dramatic pink and purple kaleidoscope of dusk provided the last glimpses of light, the two men returned home in their carriage.

"I was very impressed with the younger daughter. Do you think I could have a chance?" Bautista shyly asked his friend, almost ashamed to bring up such a topic at this completely inappropriate moment. "Is there any way that, in a few days, you could help me arrange a visit with her?" he asked.

Mateo, looking at his friend, produced a big smile, did not answer but kept guiding the carriage through the rocky road. However, a few days later, Mateo did arrange the visit.

Eight months later, on February 14, 1920, Maria walked down the aisle of her village's Catholic Church. Bautista, wearing his best attire and looking as handsome as a movie star, was waiting anxiously at the altar beside his best friend, Mateo. The bride wore a simple black dress in observance of the mourning for her mother's recent death.

Figure 1. Maria and Bautista Castañer's Wedding. February 14, 1920.

Soon after their wedding, Bautista and Maria embarked on a trip to Cuba, searching for the future they envisioned for themselves and to form a family. Spain had succumbed to an abysmal economic situation. It was common for young people to travel to Cuba in search of a brighter future. One million two hundred Spanish immigrants arrived in Cuba between 1902 and 1928.[7]

Bautista brought his life savings, which he had accumulated through long hours of hard work, in his homeland. As soon as they arrived in Cuba, they were taken by an acquaintance of the family to the area of the island called Oriente, in the eastern part of Cuba.

In 1921, with the modest funds they brought with them, Bautista was able to purchase a small coffee plantation in Arroyo de la Güira, near the Sierra Maestra Mountain range. The property was located on the top of a luscious green hill and bordered by a creek at the bottom of the slope. They built a modest home with a barn, and Bautista cultivated the land while Maria raised chickens. The land was fertile, and the soil was rich in nutrients, yielding a rich harvest. Annually, Bautista hired workers to harvest the coffee. The same workers returned every season.

There was only one harvest per year, lasting two to three months from September to March. Coffee was picked by hand. Workers selectively collected only the ripe coffee beans, then returned to the tree several times over a period of a few weeks to pick the remaining ones as they ripened. On average, pickers would gather between a hundred and two hundred pounds of coffee beans daily. Of this, only about twenty percent was retained as the best coffee.

During this time, Bautista and the laborers worked non-stop from sunrise to sunset. The coffee beans were placed in coffee driers on long row sections of zinc layers.

When Bautista shouted, "Rain is coming!" The workers would run to the driers to cover the containers and protect the beans. When the skies cleared, the trays were uncovered, and the beans spread out with rakes to continue drying. The dried coffee was placed in hefty sacs to be sold. Every year, their plantation harvested and sold dozens of sacs of excellent quality coffee.

Cuba's soil was known as a remarkably fertile soil for coffee, sugar cane, and many other crops.[8]

In 1920, a year after establishing themselves on this new land, Maria gave birth to their firstborn, Alfredo. The couple was fortunate enough to retain the region's midwife to assist Maria during her delivery in their modest home. A year later, their first daughter, Aurora, was born. Roman, the second son, arrived shortly after. Lastly, on May 14, 1925, Enedina, the fourth child, was born.

Figure 2. The Castañer Family.

Not too far away from the family lived Carmen, one of Bautista's sisters who, following her brother's footsteps, had arrived from Spain, and moved with her family into a small barn nearby. The children called her *Tía Carmen* - Aunt Carmen.

"Tía Carmen is too heavy, and that's because she sits in that rocking chair on her front porch all day long, all hours of the day," Five-year-old Enedina said, laughing and joking about her aunt.

"She is keeping an eye on her kids, Pepe, and Nina. They play with you and your brothers and sister outside," Maria responded. "I'm grateful because I must work. So, she is also looking after you."

With laughter in her voice, she responded, "No, she is not! She is only rocking herself back and forth."

The four siblings and cousins joyfully played in the luscious open green fields among hills, creeks, and valleys, only scared by an old, worn-down barn nearby. As far as they could remember, the old barn had been dark and empty for as long as they lived on the farm. Rumors circulated among the kids that the barn was haunted, but no one had ever dared to walk inside.

"If you don't do as we tell you, we are going to tie you up and lock you inside the haunted barn!" In fun, the boys often enjoyed scaring the girls.

"No!" Enedina and Aurora screamed and ran away at this creepy thought. The boys had the time of their lives laughing at the girls' fearful reactions.

An ancient communication road, which started in la Punta de Maisí and ended in El Cabo de San Antonio, called El Camino Real, was the main highway in the area. Horses and carriages used this road, connecting the farms with the nearest towns. On one side of the road lay a torn-up massive tank once used for corn storage.

In 1924, the earliest officially classified Category 5 hurricane made landfall in Cuba[9] and dropped the corn tank in the middle of El Camino Real. Dr. Luzon, the only physician who would dare travel to the area, inquired about it.

"No one has been able to move it out of the way," commented Bautista.

"It's in the middle of the road!" Replied Dr. Luzon.

"I know. That tank has been on the road for as long as we've lived here."

Dr. Luzon occasionally visited families living in the mountains of this region. Good Spanish food and wine sparked a great friendship between the doctor and the Castañer family. Bautista and Maria treated the doctor with typical fare: Spanish ham, cheese, chickpea stew, and excellent Rioja wine.

"This is the best part of my travels. It gives me the energy to continue." Dr. Luzon would enjoy this delicious resting stop at the Castañer home.

In the evening, after a hard day's work and dinner, when the kids had gone to bed, Bautista appreciated his well-deserved Cuban cigar.

A few years later, Bautista commented to his wife, "Maria, the kids need to attend school, and there are no schools in this area," realizing that the kids were growing up and needed an education. "The farm could sustain our expenses if we move away," he added. "Miguel is an honest man. He can run the plantation and send us the harvest money wherever we are."

Their coffee plantation was profitable, and Miguel Pons,

the foreman of the plantation, was a reliable, hard-working, and honest man who assisted Bautista. He was able to run the plantation on his own.

"What are you thinking, Bautista?" Maria replied.

"Let's go back to our homeland! We both miss family, we miss our country, we miss our roots." Maria's face reflected a fusion of surprise, emotion, worry, and joy.

"I don't know Bautista. Yes, I miss my family and would love to see them again, but our home is here now." She paced in a circle, and every step echoed her inner turmoil, shaking at the prospect of the new idea.

"We have four small kids, and you know how terrible the economic situation is in Spain.[10] Our family thinks that we are so lucky to be here. People are starving back home, scrounging for work. Spain is in a terrible depression."

Bautista, grabbing her gently by the arms, tried to calm her down. "But we would not need to work. We would receive enough money from this plantation to live a modest but comfortable life and provide the kids a good education."

After weeks of reflection, Bautista and Maria prepared for their return to Spain. They packed, purchased the tickets to travel, gave instructions to Miguel Pons, and left Cuba. The family of six boarded *The Cristobal Colon*, an enormous passenger vessel that every year carried thousands of passengers between Cuba and Spain, with a stop to refuel in New York.

In August of 1930, the family made port in Bilbao, located on the northern coast of Spain, close to the border with France. After disembarking, they boarded a train bound for Mas de las Matas, the hometown that cradled Bautista's formative years.

Zaragoza, across the Ebro River from Mas de las Matas, was the nearest city with a bank where Bautista could receive the profits from his Cuban coffee plantation.

The kids were enrolled in the best school in the area, and for the next six years, they lived an unassuming but happy life.

In the early months of 1936, Bautista resolved to journey back to Cuba to personally attend to the oversight of his plantation. He entrusted the care of Maria and their four children to a cousin whose husband had been called to serve in the war. Upon reaching Cuba, Bautista discovered that the plantation operated with seamless efficiency and marked success. Miguel Pons, the steward who had overseen the plantation since 1920, proved himself to be an ethical and genuinely good man.

Bautista felt confident in making a permanent return to Spain, and within a month, he embarked on the familiar vessel, the *Cristobal Colon*, the same ship that had carried him and his family six years prior. However, this time, he encountered a very different Spain.

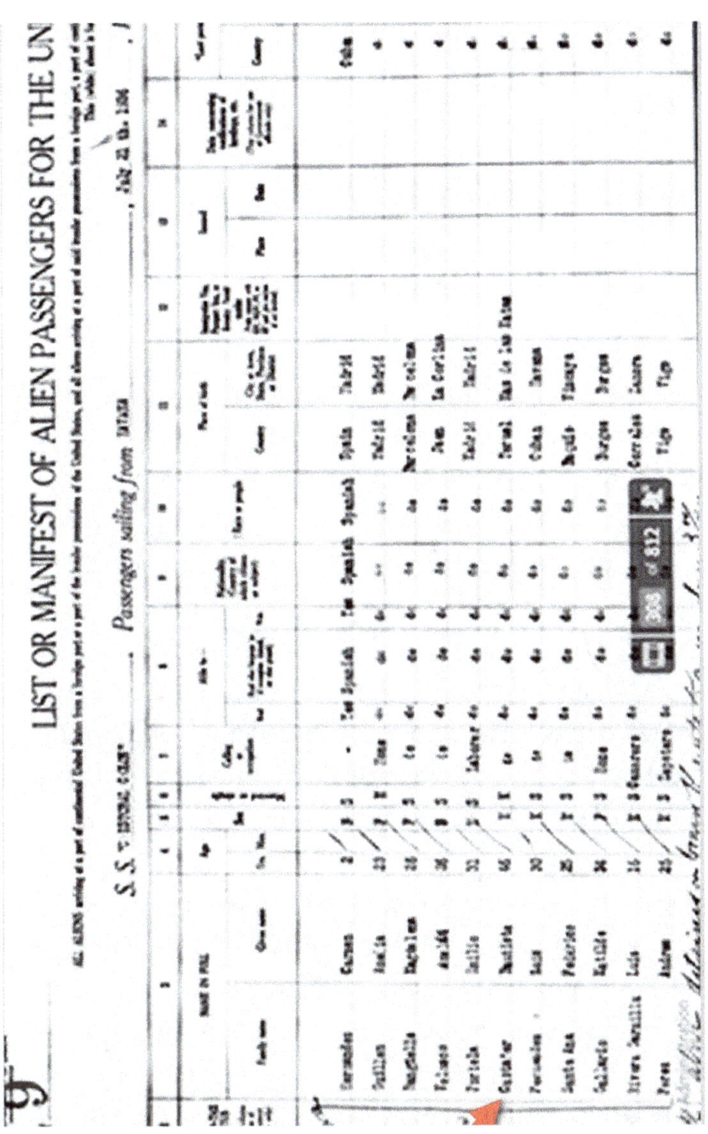

Figure 3. List of passengers showing Bautista Castañer aboard the Cristobal Colon. July 21, 1936.

3

FLEEING FROM WAR FRONTS

Port of Bilbao, Spain
1936

A dramatic swoosh followed an ear-shattering explosive glass sound in the air. The energy of the impact propelled humans and objects from the boat ramp into the water and the dock as the last passengers of *The Cristobal Colon* were projected from the ship, which had recently docked at the Port of Bilbao.

Shocked, distressed, stunned by the explosion, and not realizing what had happened, Bautista ended up face down on the rough cement. His face was battered and scratched by the impact against the concrete dock. Confused and dizzy, he struggled to stand up. *Am I dead? Alive? Awake? Asleep? What just happened?* His eyes searched in the direction of the thunderous impact, only to see the dreadful cloud of smoke rising behind him. A bomb detonated by anarchists had blown up the ship, sinking his lifetime belongings, everything he was bringing back from Cuba.

These were disturbing times in Spain; the political uprisings and the multiple leftist and rightist parties created the horrors of one of the bloodiest wars in history. A process of political polarization had characterized the Spanish Second Republic, and party divisions became increasingly embittered.

News of the rightist military coup in July 1936 unleashed a social revolutionary response, and no leftist region escaped revolutionary and anticlerical violence. Tens of thousands of people, including Roman Catholic priests, were brutally killed, and there were attacks as well on the Spanish nobility, industrialists, and conservative politicians. Particularly tragic was the desecration and burning of monasteries and churches. A revolt by the Nationalists, an alliance of Falangists, monarchists, conservatives, and Catholics, led by a military group within which General Francisco Franco soon achieved a preponderant role, initiated the Civil War.

"Are you ok? Are you hurt?" A concerned, compassionate individual was assisting those who were wounded but alive.

"Let's get out of here! Come on! Move! Move!"

Agonizing screams filled the air. Those familiar with the horrors of war were helping others and rushing them to move out of the area. As the passengers recovered from the impact, some were hurt by the projectile pieces from the explosion, and some, ripped by the pain of losing their precious possessions, helped each other as best they could. The shaken and ailing group, thankful to be alive, tried to compose themselves to escape the dangerous explosive site.

Bautista watched, speechless.

Our documents, wedding pictures, and the personal items that we acquired with so much effort in our first few years of marriage. Gone! Blown to pieces! Drifting to the bottom of the ocean.

He sighed.

He had brought all their precious belongings with him with the dream of permanently relocating back to Spain. At that moment, he could not have fathomed that this was only the beginning of a lifetime of recurring exiles and losses due to war.

The disheartened group carried whatever items were salvaged and helped each other while heading away from the pier to a safer spot.

"The war has started!" someone shouted. "The main roads west and south, all closed."

"Heavy shelling surrounds the area, and most forms of transportation are closed." Amidst the chaos, these were the resonating voices. "The only way out of here is to circumvent the war zones into the monstrous mountain range of the Pyrenees. Once out of here and into the Pyrenees, a path back into the center of the peninsula could be found." Someone from the group shouted.

If I could get to Barcelona, I have family there. They will be able to help me return home, Bautista thought.

Each member in this group who'd escaped the explosion anxiously experienced their own story.

Walking away, saddened by what they had gone through and helping each other out, they could not grasp the terrible situation in which they found their homeland. They could only think of how to return to the families they had left behind.

The group of passengers impacted by the explosion, soon began the exhausting days' journey, hiking through the arid hills of the Pyrenees. The nights were bitterly cold. It was easy to get lost wandering through valleys, hills, heavy mist, and massive mountains. And always, the fear of encountering a stray bullet from the militia stayed with them. It was difficult to move quietly on those hillsides among the crackling shrubs and tinkling limestone.

Stomachs growled, food was scarce, and bodies fell and rose again. The group continued their journey, day, and night, only stopping as dusk approached and their bodies could not endure anymore. To cushion their bodies overnight, in any open safe area or amid the woods, they arranged the shawls, coats, clothing, or bags they had salvaged on the ground. As soon as the first rays of sunshine appeared on the horizon, the group packed up and continued their endless trek.

In nearby Huesca, the fronts were fighting, posing an immediate danger to this area. After twenty-seven non-stop, exhausting, long days of walking with little time for rest, *¡Al fin!* – finally, they arrived in the city of Barcelona, which sat as a mirage at the end of the desert. However, their anxiously awaited destination had sadly become a war hot spot.

Pascual, Bautista's cousin, who resided in Barcelona, provided him with food, clean clothing, and a resting place and assisted him with the development of a plan to reach his family in Mas de las Matas.

The experiences Batista had encountered, enhanced by his yearning to reach his family, transformed his personality into that of a fearless man.

As he arrived in Barcelona, news about the August 14, 1936, bloody Battle of Badajoz invaded the radio waves. However, he was relieved to know that his family was much closer, only 131 miles from Barcelona and, for now, at least, away from the war fronts. Two days later, Bautista departed for Zaragoza, hoping to cross the Ebro River to reach his destination.

The constant news of the dangers and atrocities of the

war, on top of the scarcity of information from Bautista, had Maria and the kids worried about their fate.

Early on the morning of October of 1936, several months after his departure, Bautista eventually arrived to find his family in Mas de las Matas. The father and the husband, whom they had sometimes doubted ever seeing again, returned safely. Bautista, surrounded by his family, looked extremely thin and exhausted but blissful after surviving one of the greatest ordeals of his life.

"Dad!"

"Bautista!"

"Dad, we were so worried that we often questioned your safe return." They said, between tears and hugs, "We never lost hope. We are so grateful that you are finally here!"

Upon his arrival, the family felt temporarily safe and, for a while, enjoyed the sheltered and wonderful feeling of their reunion once again.

4

ANTONIO

- AN ACT OF KINDNESS AND BRAVERY
Mas de las Matas, Teruel to Cheste, Valencia.
November 1936

Antonio screamed, "You all have to leave. I'll be executed on the spot if I'm caught here, but I have to save you, my family!"

"Let's go! There is no time to waste. The militias are moving in this direction. They will burn down the town, rape the women, kill hundreds, leaving only destruction behind." Panic painted on Antonio's face as he stormed into the house that the Castañer family had called home for the last six years.

On that crisp morning in November of 1936, Antonio, Maria's nephew who was a soldier of the revolutionary militia, stormed into his aunt's family home to alert them of the imminent danger. Although worried for the boys, Antonio could not fathom what could happen to the women of his family, Maria and her two daughters, thirteen-year-old Aurora, and eleven-year-old Enedina. The militia was notorious for the rape and savage treatment of hundreds of women. During this time, if lucky, citizens of small towns were alerted when either the Nationalist or the Republican armies were advancing in their direction. Families were forced to move out immediately, leaving all their belongings behind. The two armies confronted each other throughout the country, bringing destruction and death to those already impoverished towns.

For the last few months, the war enveloped the family within the limits of the Ebro River. Famine overcame the nation as well as Bautista's family. They no longer had access to their savings in Zaragoza since passage had become impossible.

"I need to pack some things!" Maria cried, with four children's faces staring in utter fear at Antonio.

"Let's go!" shouted Antonio.

"Let's go!" Bautista echoed the frenzied words, reacting immediately. "We barely have time to get the kids ready for days of long treks to who knows where."

Antonio loaded the four children into the cargo bed of his old truck in between large mounds of straw, where the girls held on tightly to each other, attempting to hide their fragile, trembling bodies. Betrayed by the anxious expressions on their faces, Alfredo and Roman, the two slim, handsome young boys, struggled with self-control. Bautista and Maria rode with Antonio in the front.

Trying to avoid the attention of passersby, Antonio drove several miles southeast from Mas de las Matas, as far away from the war fronts as he could. He had cautioned the children, "If you see militias approaching, hide underneath the straw."

Not long into their journey, Antonio said, "I cannot go any further. I must go back."

Abandoning the militia to save his family could be considered an act of treason. He knew that if caught, he would be labeled a deserter.

"This part of the journey is safer than our initial route. Keep walking until you reach a secure town where you can spend the night."

Maria, with tears in her eyes, embraced Antonio, thanking him for his heroic and selfless action. "Please, take care of yourself. We want you alive. Come back to us."

Antonio sped back to the war front while the family pressed on with their journey on foot. The children were tired and hungry; they had no food and nowhere to stay. That night, scared and trembling, they hid in a concealed grove to get some sleep, engulfed by the shadows of the trees.

"Maria, I must find something for our children to eat," Bautista whispered as the first rays brightened the horizon. The kids were still asleep from the exhaustion of the previous day.

Fearful and penniless but with a sense of urgency, Bautista left determined to find food for his family. He walked toward nearby farms, on alert to avoid guard dogs, until he spotted a relatively open crop field not far away. He stole a few vegetables, mostly sweet potatoes and legumes, packing as much as he could carry, knowing that this may be the only meal his kids would eat for the day.

On his return to the hidden spot, he found them all awake, eagerly awaiting any amount of food. The children approached him with their healthy appetites; the boys' eyes sparked gratefully. They were so hungry that each one grabbed a portion and devoured it immediately, barely removing the dirt from the load. The women, starving but abiding by their cultural deference to their men, allowed the boys the greater part of the feast.

Shaking off leaves, grass, and straw from their dirty

clothes, they immediately got ready to continue. They walked all day, tirelessly retreating from battlefronts, in the direction of a safe spot to spend the following night.

"Hide! Everyone, hide, they must not see us!" Bautista shouted to alert his family of the warplanes flying overhead. As the sky turned grey, the shadows engulfed the escapees hiding beneath the canopy of trees.

"Run!"

They could hear the rumbling of the bombs falling in the distance, shaking the earth not far away. Overnight, military planes continued their missions, and sporadic bombings continued. The ground shook and then stilled. Finally, only dark silence prevailed.

"We need to keep moving away from the war front." Bautista directed in a frenzy. The boys looked up with anxiety but also with excitement in their eyes. Enedina and Aurora, however, gazed at the skies with visible panic. Although they could not grasp the dire gravity of the situation, they knew they could not be afraid. They were raised to be strong against all odds. Trembling in their hiding space and holding tight to each other, they spent the night in an uneasy sleep of exhaustion, feeling the quaking earth and listening to the thunderous noise of the bombs.

Bautista, waking at dawn, left in an ongoing attempt to find food for his family. He intended to steal more legumes and maybe some potatoes from a nearby farm. Two wolf-like dogs suddenly appeared and barked fiercely, alerting the owners. With the sounds of shots heading his way, Bautista, at forty-three, suddenly energized into a much younger, more athletic young man, jumping and running, hoping to outrun the bullets. That day, the family would not eat; they continued their long and harrowing walk on empty stomachs.

After several difficult days of hunger, long hikes, and hiding, they finally reached the small town of Cheste in Valencia, where they settled safely until the end of the war in 1939.

Figure 4. Castañer Family: First row, Maria, and Bautista, second row from left to right, Aurora, Alfredo C (Gallego), Roman and Enedina.

Figure 5. Extended Castañer family, including spouses and grandchildren.

5

GALICIAN STOWAWAY

*From Santiago de Compostela, Galicia
to Santiago de Cuba, Cuba.
1903*

Paco Barrio was visiting his brother Manuel one afternoon and informed him in secrecy about his plans. "I'm leaving Spain. And please don't say anything to our sisters, Rita and Consuelo, until after my departure."

In 1903, in Santiago de Compostela, Galicia, the five Barrio siblings, ranging in age from six to eleven, lost their mother, who was their remaining parent. Paco, the older brother, followed by Manuel, Maximo, Rita, and Consuelo, all ended up in separate foster care.

"*Pero hermano* - brother, how would you manage to stowaway on a ship? What will happen to you if they catch you and discover your plan?"

"Don't worry," he said, his eyes shining with the excitement of his upcoming adventure. "This is not a crazy, impetuous idea. I've been thinking and planning this for a while." He added. "I've heard so many success stories. I cannot continue locked up in this orphanage."

Paco, a vivacious young boy eager to go far in life, went on, "Every time I can, I escape from the orphanage and walk by the port to observe the cargo ships that leave every week. It will not be hard. I can easily sneak in when no one is

27

watching."

"But it takes several weeks to reach Cuba. What would you eat? How would you survive?" Manuel responded, worried about his brother's fate.

"I'll figure it out," Paco said, "I'll steal food from the kitchen at night when no one is watching and will save it to eat while I travel." The more challenges Manuel raised, the greater the excitement on Paco's face. "Don't worry *hermano*, the worst that could happen is that they send me back and throw me in jail for a while. I'm still a minor, so they can't do much."

In the early 1900s, the world was in the grips of a stowaway craze. As long as there has been transportation to faraway places, people sneaked on board. However, the illicit act didn't have a name in English until 1848, when "stowaway" entered the language. By the end of the nineteenth century, stowaways had become a regular feature of immigration to America's Eastern Seaboard. The stowaway fad was so popular that many youngsters saw it as an adventure.

Using an old, ragged sack, Paco packed his only other shorts, shirt, underwear, and the food he had been able to steal or save from his regular meals. On a cold and cloudy September morning, before dawn, before workers reported, Paco quietly sneaked out of the orphanage toward the nearby Port of Bilbao. Carefully gazing left, right, back, and left again while swiftly walking to make sure not to be seen, Paco headed toward the port. His eyes sparkled with fearless excitement.

Dawn started to break, and silence prevailed. No one was up this early. Eagerness filled his soul at the first sight of the ship, which he had been watching for several days.

First, as planned, he stopped in a hidden corner, then bent down and stooped low. He ran carefully from one hiding spot to the next. Panting, he stopped and looked around, bending some more. His skinny body was able to hide behind even the smallest object. He kept moving until, finally, he arrived at the ramp through which he had planned to enter the ship. He crouched and ran rapidly down the ramp. As he reached the end of the ramp, he turned right to hide behind a huge box and stopped to catch his breath. Then, more steps. He finally spotted the steps that would eventually lead him to his final dim, secluded corner in the cargo area.

Not seeing anyone around, he took his time to explore the area in search of a safe place where he would tuck in to spend the next thirty to forty-five days. He didn't even know precisely how many days he was going to be confined to his hiding spot. Trembling from cold, fear, and hunger, Paco was eager to find a better life for himself and his siblings on the promised paradise island called Cuba.

Paco was not the only one looking for a better life on the island. During the first decade of the twentieth century, Cuba experienced a wave of immigrants from various countries, including Syria, Palestine, Lebanon, Poland, India, Japan, Sweden, Finland, and Spain. It was believed that Cuban elites promoted immigration to "whiten" a country they feared had become "too black" after the 1895-1898 Cuban War of Independence from Spain. Spaniards like Paco, mainly from the Galicia region of the country, viewed Cuba as a hopeful destination since Spain was transitioning through a severe recession and on the brink of a civil revolution.

He arrived in Santiago de Cuba, the second largest city on the island, a beautiful colonial town on the eastern end of Cuba, nestled in a valley of the Sierra Maestra, pierced by a pouch-shaped bay on the Caribbean Sea, and one which embraced many Spanish immigrants in the early 1900s. It was a prosperous place for hard-working immigrants.

"How much would you pay me if I fix these chairs for you?" Paco asked one day as he walked the streets of Santiago de Cuba in search of food to quiet his hunger.

"Hey, kid, go away! Those are broken beyond repair," replied a man who was discarding a dining set.

"Please, let me take them. I think I can repair them," Paco offered.

"Take them if you want, but don't bring them back," said the man.

Paco had learned some wood turning back in Spain. So, he took the chairs to the shelter where he was staying. "Tomorrow, I'll work on them," he told himself.

A week later, he returned to the home of the discarded furniture with one of the chairs repaired and varnished.

"Kid, you are good!" The man had to admit despite himself. "How did you manage to create this beauty? An amazing transformation! Julia, come over, see what this kid did." As Julia walked out the door of her house, she was astonished by what she saw,

"Is that my chair?" she asked. "I told you, Pepe, that those could be refurbished. It's beautiful!"

"Would you like me to do the same with the other five?" Paco paused to observe their reaction.

"Yes!" Julia responded with enthusiasm.

"Then, you will have to give me some *pesos* – money, now to buy materials to work on the other ones." Paco waited for the answer from the grumpy old man and the bubbly wife.

"Yes, Pepe, give him what he is asking for. I want my beautiful chairs back."

The old man wrinkled his face in disgust at what he was about to say. "How much do you need to refurbish the other ones?" His words ejected from his mouth.

"Well, I need to buy screws, sandpaper, and varnish. Varnish is expensive, you know!"

"How about five pesos?" The old man said while extracting the money from his pocket.

"Six." Paco paused with a grin on his face. "And are you going to pay me for the finished one I brought back today?"

"No. I'll pay you when you finish all of them." Paco jumped back out of fear at the old man's loud, angry voice. He took the five pesos from the old man's hand and left, running off announcing, "I'll be back with the other chairs in a few days."

"Make sure that you don't steal my money. I will find you wherever you hide, and I will make you pay!"

Paco was shocked but smiled at the irritability of the old man. He left, running invigorated with happiness, knowing he had made his first great business deal. The strong breeze tossed his curly hair as he ran and jumped, exhilarated, toward his boarding house, immersed in thought, walking, tilting against the wind of dusk. An early full moon emerged behind a cloud, and Paco felt blessed.

6
JACOBA AND THE ORPHAN BOY
Santiago de Compostela, Spain.
1906-1914

Five years later, Paco's brother, thirteen-year-old Manuel, managed to escape from the orphanage where he had spent the last few years. Clad in ragged clothing, he traversed the streets of Santiago de Compostela, exhausted, sweaty, and famished. His stomach growled incessantly, pleading for nourishment. With a flicker of hope he ventured forward, hoping to find employment that would alleviate his dire circumstances.

Suddenly, a delightful fragrance wafted through the air, captivating Manuel's senses and drawing him toward a nearby store. In awe, he stood before an expansive glass window, his eyes fixed on the sight of golden, soft, and moist breads, a delectable array of pastries and sweets adorned with cascading caramel and oozing chocolate. His mouth watered, and he couldn't tear away his gaze from this enticing feast. However, the harsh reality reminded him that he had no money, no job, and, thus, no means to partake in such indulgence.

From within the store, Jacoba, the owner of the bakery, noticed Manuel and observed him for a while. Something about this boy struck a deep sense of pity in her heart.

Stepping outside, she approached Manuel and asked, "Are you hungry, my boy?"

Manuel, overcome with shame, hesitated for a few seconds before shyly nodding in affirmation.

"Come inside, my child. I will give you some food." Jacoba offered warmly.

Grateful for her kindness, Manuel replied, "Thank you. I am willing to work in exchange for the food."

Jacoba retreated to the back of the counter, the place where she served her customers, and prepared a small plate with a piece of bread and other baked goods. A spark of joy illuminated his eyes. His fingers trembled with anticipation as he cradled the nourishing gift in his hands. With each bite, he savored the flavors as if it were a long-lost treasure finally recovered. Jacoba watched him with curiosity, a knot forming in her heart. She couldn't help but see her own sons reflected in this impoverished boy.

"Thank you, ma'am! These tasted heavenly! Thank you. But please allow me to work for this meal. I can help you with various tasks, such as cleaning the floors. Please, let me prove my worth," Manuel implored.

Impressed by the boy's earnest desire to work, Jacoba regarded him and said, "You know, I truly could use some help around here." She paused, considering her words carefully. "Perhaps you could be who I need." With that, Jacoba decided to hire Manuel for the day with the intention of assessing his capabilities with chores around the store. "I will give you work today to see how it goes."

Throughout the day, Manuel toiled diligently, meticulously cleaning every surface in the store—floors, counters, ovens, whatever needed his attention. He was determined to prove his usefulness and efficiency.

That night, as Manuel showed no indication of leaving, Jacoba took notice. "Boy, where do you live?" she inquired genuinely concerned.

Reluctantly, Manuel answered, "I don't have a place to live. My parents died." He paused for a while. "My father left a long time ago. My siblings and I stayed with my mom. Then, she died."

Jacoba's response was empathetic, recognizing the prevalence of such circumstances in that area during that time. "Well, stay here for the night," she offered kindly. "Tomorrow, we will figure out what to do." Jacoba allowed Manuel to shower, gave him a few of her son's clothes, and asked him to spend the night despite her husband's apprehensions.

"Jacoba, you have no knowledge of who this boy is. He could be a thief, for all we know."

"But look at him. He is just a poor, homeless boy. He isn't a thief. Besides, he spent the entire day working hard to earn the food I provided." She defended the boy.

Over the next seven years, Manuel found solace and a sense of belonging within Jacoba's family. He regarded her as the mother he had lost, although Jacoba's husband remained somewhat skeptical. Nonetheless, he accepted Manuel into their fold. Treated as an equal alongside her own sons, Manuel became an integral part of their family, seen as their third son.

In the broader world, the assassination of Austrian Archduke Franz Ferdinand on June 28, 1914, served as the catalyst for the commencement of World War I (WWI). Following this assassination, a series of events unfolded, leading Austria-Hungary to declare war on Serbia on July 28, 1914, marking the official beginning of WWI.[11]

Although the world had plunged into the turmoil of the war, now twenty-one-year-old Manuel remained resolute in pursuing his dream of reaching Cuba. He had managed to accumulate enough money to undertake the journey. Although Spain did not actively participate in WWI, numerous Spaniards and individuals from other countries volunteered for military service. One of Jacoba's sons enlisted as a volunteer and was deployed to a front.

Aware of Manuel's yearning to reunite with his brother in Cuba, Jacoba expressed her concern, "Manuel, I understand your eagerness to travel to Cuba and reunite with your brother. However, the world is in a state of crisis. Traveling under such circumstances can be perilous."

"I have to go, *Madre* - Mother," He would call her *Madre* because of the love and care she had given him. "I have to start my life. I must go now." Manuel said, trying to describe his feelings of urgency. He was at a point in his life where he felt he could not wait any longer, regardless of all external challenges.

Jacoba had seen him save every penny he could throughout the years to fulfill his dream. Now he had enough money to travel and survive for a while until he settled in the new land. The conflict was obstructing his plans and made him feel like a caged tiger, roaming around, looking for a way to get through the bars and back onto his planned path to freedom.

"I have been told that to embark, I need a new type of document called a passport. I don't have any credentials to apply for such a document—I'm an orphan. I don't have any documents." Passports had not generally been required for international travel until the first world war,[12] but it was required at this time.

Despondent, Manuel walked out of the bakery. Jacoba could not sleep that night, tossing in bed, wondering how she could help Manuel. The next day, as he walked into the store, she said, "I need to talk to you in private. Meet me in the back of the store."

"Manuel, I was pondering an idea all night." She looked at him, wondering if she should continue. "Your brother, who left for the war, left his passport behind. As a military volunteer, he was not required to take it with him." She stopped to gaze at the light in Manuel's eyes. He knew what she was thinking. "He is about your age and height, and his looks and yours are somewhat similar."

"*Madre*, are you implying that maybe I could use his passport?"

She nodded hesitantly in affirmation. "We cannot tell *Papá* - Dad. He will not approve."

Manuel embraced Jacoba with tears in his eyes and said, "You have always been so good to me."

Manuel left elated, floating on air, while in his mind forging plans to leave.

Manuel groomed himself, mostly his hair, to look as much as possible like his brother's picture in the passport and bought the ticket for the next passenger ship to Cuba. Travel had slowed because of the war and the possible danger encountered by commercial vessels in international waters.

Initially, when the German U-boats or submarines met merchant ships, they surfaced before they attacked and allowed those onboard time to escape. However, from February 1915, the Germans changed their tactics. U-boats began to fire on ships without warning—including neutral and passenger vessels.[13]

There were rumors that vessels off the North Carolina coast had been sunk by German U-boats. They had managed to sink ten vessels and 200 American ships in total.[14]

Manuel's journey to Cuba was fraught with uncertainty and danger. Despite his excitement and determination to start a new life, the events of WWI cast a shadow over his plans.

As Manuel boarded the ship, his immediate concern was the authenticity of his borrowed passport. He had taken great care to resemble Jacoba's son in appearance, hoping to pass the scrutiny of any suspicious eyes.

Thankfully, his impersonation worked, and he managed to board the vessel without encountering any complications.

However, that night turned out to be the scariest of his life when the perils of the open seas soon became apparent. Manuel and his fellow passengers were informed that the ship had to sail in complete darkness to evade detection by enemy warships. The fear of being mistaken for a hostile vessel and targeted by torpedoes gripped everyone on board. Nights became sleepless, and anxiety permeated the air as they braved the unknown waters of the sea.

Weeks turned into a blur of fear and anticipation as Manuel sailed toward his destination. The journey, once envisioned as a stepping stone toward his dreams, had become a test of resilience and fortitude. Manuel's determination to reunite with his brother and start afresh in Cuba remained steadfast, providing a glimmer of hope amid the tumultuous backdrop of war.

The serene expanse of the Atlantic Ocean appeared remarkably tranquil, providing a stark contrast to the harrowing conflicts raging across the globe.

7

ROMANTIC ENCOUNTER
Guantanamo and Santiago de Cuba.
1916

After a long and terrifying journey, Manuel finally arrived safely at the port of Havana. From there, he traveled to Santiago de Cuba, where he reunited with his brother Paco, who was in the early stages of building his own small furniture store.

Over time, all the Barrio-Costolla siblings managed to escape Spain to reunite in Cuba, except Rita, who found her new home in Argentina.

Along with his wife, Maria Viel-Suarez, in Santiago de Cuba, Paco offered Manuel lodging in a small room at the rear of the store. Manuel joined his brother, working diligently to advance Paco's furniture store.

One evening, shortly after Manuel's arrival, a sense of excitement filled the air as Maria eagerly announced at home, "My little sister America is coming this evening to visit us. I would like for you, Manuel, to meet her."

Unbeknownst to anyone, Maria had matchmaking plans in mind for her younger sister, America, who was in her twenties. That evening, Manuel, whose difficult life up to that point had given him no time to think about his personal life, was captivated by America's cute petite figure and personality. He watched her quietly while admiring her

39

beautiful, long, reddish hair and peculiar French features. He was not accustomed to seeing women like her. Meanwhile, in the kitchen, while preparing dinner, America admitted in a gasp to her sister, "He is handsome, with those dazzling green eyes and light auburn hair," Her eyes glinted with a fleeting glimmer of delight.

"He is so different from the men around here. I really like him. I hope he likes me too."

That night, as America bid her farewell, Manuel's face lit up with a radiant smile as he sought solace in his brother's company, "I think I like her. I would love to see her again." Both brothers grinned. Something special was brewing.

8
AMERICA'S GROWING YEARS
Guantanamo
1900s

Guantanamo Bay had been historically significant due to its strategic location and unique topographic features, attracting the interest of maritime powers since the fifteenth century. Christopher Columbus landed at the Bay on his second voyage to the New World, and it later became a contested territory among the empires of England, France, and Spain. In 1898, the United States took control of the Bay, along with their Cuban allies, using it as a forward-operating base in their effort to challenge Spanish control of the island.[15]

In 1903, Cuba signed an indefinite treaty granting the exclusive use of Guantanamo Bay to the U.S. for naval or coal mining purposes.[16]

Alejandro Viel worked as a coal miner and served as the sole source of income for the family. His job demanded long and grueling hours, toiling in harsh mining conditions.

In the absence of both parents, the older siblings stepped up to assume parental responsibilities, particularly Pastora, the oldest sister, who took on a motherly role for the younger children, including two-year-old America, whom she practically raised after their mother died.

Recognizing the importance of education, the older

siblings decided to initiate reading and writing classes for the younger ones. With the few books that they could find, they started an in-home education program. Other disciplines were later added. As word spread, neighboring families joined for the benefit of their children. One by one, the program grew rapidly, giving birth to an elementary school.

Due to the fast pace of their initiative, they saw the need to order books and even asked the younger siblings to assist with teaching.

The absence of knowledge did not stop them from doing their duties. Each evening, after dinner, the small home transformed into a makeshift library, with the younger ones seated on the floor while the older sisters were at the dinner table. The room was filled with books covering various subjects, including reading, writing, mathematics, history, and art. Everyone eagerly absorbed knowledge from the books while the older sisters coordinated assignments and the delivery of instruction. Each sibling mastered a specific topic, preparing to pass on their newfound knowledge to the students the following day.

"All that I learned, I learned by teaching." America, the youngest child, would claim later in life.

9

THE EMPEROR OF THE FOLDING CHAIRS

Santiago de Cuba
1919

Three years after Manuel and America's romantic encounter, on April 18, 1919, Manuel Barrio-Costolla and America Viel-Suarez were married in Guantanamo, Cuba.

Both Maria and America, two sisters who married two brothers, were not only loving wives but also intelligent and diligent, actively supporting their husbands' business endeavors, managing household chores, and assisting at the furniture store.

After their wedding, Manuel and America lived in a tiny room at the back of Paco's store, where their first son, Pucho, was born prematurely.

Figure 6. *Manuel Barrio Costoya and America Viel Suarez, 1919.*

43

Following a work-related disagreement with Paco and America, being pregnant with their second child prompted them to seek alternative housing for the growing family. "America, I'm heading to my sister Consuelo to see if she can accommodate us in their home temporarily, at least until the baby is born."

America patted her pregnant belly, and a loving smile lit her face. She wanted to soften his level of stress caused by the recent events.

That evening, Manuel encountered another challenge as he related his dilemma to his sister Consuelo, "Brother," she responded, "the only spot that I can offer you right now is in the barn where I keep my hens. I will clean a section as much as I can." Knowing how stressed her brother was, she strove to be helpful with the humble resources she could offer. "I will bring a midwife who lives nearby to assist with the delivery."

Disheartened but resolved, Manuel decided to move on with the only option available. As he arrived home, he sat in front of his wife and reaching out for her hand he said, "America, I'm so sorry that this is happening now. I could not find anything else; we don't have enough money saved to get a space anywhere else. Do you mind if my sister cleans and prepares the barn for us?" He did not wait for her response but impressed upon her. "There is really no time, and we need to act fast."

On December 21, 1922, at five o'eight in the afternoon, America, with the assistance of the midwife, delivered 8-pound Alfredo, in this humble setting, reminiscent of the birth of Jesus Christ. In a barn, in a manger, surrounded by animals but cuddled by the love of two devoted parents offering unconditional love beyond any material shortcoming.

Determined to build a better future, Manuel tirelessly worked until he could afford a small section of a building on the streets of Enramada and Padre Pico. Here, he laid the foundation for his envisioned furniture store.

"One day the building will be mine and I will have the largest furniture store in all of Santiago de Cuba." He exclaimed proudly when he brought his family to see the site. A small apartment in the back became their humble home for the next few years. The financial restrictions of the times were swathed by the peace and joy of a loving family.

Figure 7. Manuel Barrio and America Viel with sons Pucho and Alfredo.

No one ever heard them arguing. Manuel, a loving husband and father, always supported his wife, "I will not save you," he would confess to his children. "If your mom punished you, it is for a reason, and I'm with her on that."

Just one discrepancy between America and Manuel was ever heard, "Manuel, I need to cut my hair. It's too long for my age. Women my age don't wear their hair this long anymore."

But Manuel would kindly disagree, "No, no, no. I love your long hair. Please don't cut your beautiful hair."

America took good care of her husband and children, the cooking, cleaning, and all other home chores. As a smart woman, she was capable to efficiently manage both home and store adeptly in Manuel's absence.

Figure 8. Pilar Barrio.

In 1928, their first baby girl, Pilar, was born in this home. The Barrio-Viel siblings, Pucho, Alfredo, and Pilar forged in this modest home their sweetest childhood memories.

With time and hard work, Manuel managed to purchase the entire building.

Figure 9. Muebleria Barrio, Santiago de Cuba.

By the 1950s, he achieved remarkable success as the proprietor of Santiago de Cuba's largest furniture store. Notably, a significant segment of his business thrived on equipment rentals and folding chairs, a venture that garnered him the prestigious nickname of *The Emperor of the Folding Chairs.*

Figure 10. Newspaper clip advertising The Emperor of the Folding Chairs.

Despite their financial success, the couple retained their frugal mindset, "America, let's travel now that we can afford it." Manuel suggested one day.

"But some hotels and restaurants are too expensive,"

America replied. "Barrio," she used to call him by his last name, "we can buy bread, ham, and cheese and make sandwiches for dinner in our hotel room. Restaurants are too expensive."

In this way, the Barrio-Viel family built a successful life through hard work, perseverance, and resourcefulness, cherishing their humble beginnings even as they attained prosperity. Never at this point would they or anyone else have imagined that the dragon of darkness would wipe their efforts, their dreams, and their lives away.

10

PAPÁ, PAPÁ, MATE A MARIANO
DAD, DAD I KILLED MARIANO
Santiago de Cuba
1926-1930

The improvised schoolroom of Ms. Pilar Repilado was the kindergarten classroom that Alfredo attended. The room in the modest home of the Repilado family was small, simple, colorful, and bright. In the morning, the sunlight filtered like a rainbow through two small windows, providing the light needed for the twelve students who attended this class.

Each day, the six-year-olds would take their seat in one of the four chairs available at each of the three tiny tables in the room. Pilar, who happened to have the same name as Alfredo's sister, was the beautiful young daughter of the Repilado family. Pilar Repilado's mother assisted her with the students in the classroom. Although she taught under very simple and plain conditions, the colors, the brightness, and the loving instruction of Pilar were enough to impact her students. Pilar planted in Alfredo the seed of his love for learning, which stayed with him for the rest of his life.

Two years later, "¡*Niño, dónde te has metido!* - Boy, where have you been!"

"I send you out clean every morning and look at you! Go,

49

take a shower!" America shouted after seeing her muddy eight-year-old son Alfredo returning from playing in the streets.

In 1930, it was not unusual to find children playing in the streets of Santiago de Cuba. Some of the kids would play running around, chasing after one another, some with wooden sticks and crushed cans simulating Cuba's favorite sport, baseball. Alfredo, who was a robust and tough little boy, chose boxing and wrestling as his favorite sports. This explained the grimy clothing and the dusty face that was frequently seen by his mom.

Brothers Pucho and Alfredo enjoyed a child's life of play. Sometimes, their dad would ask them to help in the store carrying furniture or doing various tasks. Manuel was very strict with them, but as young kids, they enjoyed playing with all types of friends. They were raised without prejudices. Everyone was equal. Some were poorer, some had a little more money, some were white, some black, and some mulato, but all were the same to them. They were all just kids who played with whatever they could find.

"Mom, why is it that some of my friends are always barefooted?" Alfredo asked his mother one day when he realized that some of the boys he played with every day were running around either without shoes or with torn ones.

"Their parents have no money to buy them shoes," America, his mom, responded. This saddened Alfredo.

One hot and muggy afternoon, little Alfredo was playing with friends in the streets near his dad's furniture store. The boys were running in circles engrossed in their game, twirling around like tornados, unaware of their surroundings,

"Hey, you are going to hit me! Go somewhere else to

play." Mariano, a malnourished, skinny twelve-year-old boy who helped his family by running errands for people and businesses in the area, was hand-delivering a stack of boxes. Everyone in the neighborhood knew Mariano well. He was always meandering through the neighborhood attempting to land menial jobs by offering his services to the stores in the area. Foreseeing the immediate danger, Mariano yelled, "You are going to hit me, and you'll make me drop these boxes!"

Well, too late! Alfredo unintentionally collided with Mariano shaking him vigorously as if a hurricane had touched down. Boxes, tools, screws, they all came down from his arms falling in every direction of the road and Mariano himself ended up lying flat on the street.

The boys returned to look at Mariano, who appeared to be unconscious and stiff as a stick. One of the boys said to Alfredo, "I think you killed him."

"No, I did not!" Alfredo protested. Scared to death, the kids ran home in search of a safe hiding place. Alfredo worried about what he had done and ran toward his dad's furniture store down the street, yelling as he approached his dad. "¡Papá, papá, maté a Mariano! - Dad, Dad, I killed Mariano!" he cried. Shocked and perturbed about the announcement, Manuel dropped what he was doing and ran outside, following little Alfredo to the site of the event. Mariano was lying in the street surrounded by passers-by who stopped to help,

"Who knocked poor Mariano unconscious?" one of the onlookers asked while Alfredo and his dad Manuel were approaching the scene. Alfredo hid behind his father's corpulent body and frightened by the accusations and commotion in the street, he hoped that no one would discover that he was the guilty one.

"What happened? Are you ok?" Manuel asked as he moved forward to assist dizzy Mariano, who slowly stood up, recovering from his punch. Manuel dispersed the crowd. "Ok, everyone, move! I'm taking him home."

Upon arrival at the raggedy shack where Mariano and his family lived, Manuel spoke with Mariano's family, explaining and apologizing for the situation. He kindly offered to pay for all expenses, including medical, if needed. He gave the family some extra money for the inconvenience caused by the boys.

Manuel had not yet said a word to Alfredo. A light wind blew as they walked home through the dusty streets of the city. The sun was setting, and a sliver of a moon was rising in the sky.

Little Alfredo wondered, *Am I in trouble? Sure! Will I be punished for a long time?* He knew that his father, a man of few words and respected by everyone, would never place a hand on his child, but his Galician roots would emerge in his strong words.

Father and son walked side by side in a chilling silence that matched the dusk while Manuel tried to grasp his many thoughts. *I know my son is a good boy, he is just a kid, he was only playing around. How should I proceed? I know he is strong, but knocking Mariano, so much taller and older than him, unconscious. Hmm? David and Goliath? Well, poor Mariano is no Goliath,* he chuckled to himself.

"Am I going to be punished, Dad?"

"Well, I know you didn't do it on purpose, but you need to realize how strong you are and be more careful next time."

With a disguised smile on his face, eight-year-old Alfredo breathed a long sigh of relief.

11

NO MORE SCHOOL

Santiago de Cuba
1935-1943

Flustered, Manuel looked at his sons, "Ok, that's enough school for both of you. You already know how to read, write, add, subtract. What else is there to learn in school? That's enough! It's time for the two of you young men to help me with the business, and work with me full-time." Manuel continued his speech during dinner with the determined attitude that characterized the robust, grey-haired, forty-five-year-old Galician man. "I need both of you working starting tomorrow morning. No more school!"

Nothing else needed to be said. The family knew that they should only listen and follow his demands when he spoke with resolve. Any response would have been perceived as defiance. Silence persisted throughout the humble room, which they called their dining room. The solid wooden straight chairs and table crowded the tiny space with bare walls. The room was poorly lit, with a small, old, dusky picture hanging from one of the walls. The greyish walls completed the sad mood of the moment.

Fourteen-year-old Pucho and thirteen-year-old Alfredo received the news in silent grief. Pilar, being the younger and only girl, was not included in the directive. Although not completely surprised by the announcement, the boys were devastated. Alfredo loved school; he loved learning. He dreamed of learning as much as he could. He loved history, geography, political science, and mathematics. Through the sadness in their faces, they were begging their dad not to deny them further education. However, no one would dare to contradict the authoritative figure. A rare blend of dictatorship and responsibility had always been perceived as Manuel's normal behavior. A high level of respect for their father was expected from the children, and none of them would dare contradict his instructions.

Silent tears trickled down Pucho's face as he kept looking down, wiping his sadness away. "I don't want to lose my friends, my teachers. I love school, I love playing. I don't want to work, work, work in this stupid dusty place," complained Pucho to his siblings later that night.

"Shh. You don't want Dad to hear you say that. Do you think I want to drop out of school? Of course not! But do we have any other choice? This is what we must do," replied Alfredo with the same sadness in his voice.

From this moment on, the boys worked full-time at their dad's furniture store. Both, who had the burning desire to go to school, soon planned and found a way to sneak out of the house in the evenings to attend night school. They took advantage of their father's fatigue every evening after work and his habit of landing in bed early at night.

A few weeks into their nightly escapades, Alfredo questioned America. "Mom, do you think Dad has noticed that we are out every night attending night school?" The boys knew they could only ask this if their dad was not around.

"Come on!" His petite yet astute mother countered, her

visage adorned with an enigmatic expression. "Your Dad is too smart for that. I'm sure he knows but he is too proud to acknowledge defeat." She smiled at Alfredo and gave him a hug while he wriggled away from her motherly gesture.

"You know that men from Galicia and all northern Spaniards have a great heart," she continued, letting go of her son and winking at him. "He is just too stubborn to let anybody twist his arm," she added.

By sneaking out every evening, day after day, year after year, both boys were able to eventually graduate from high school. The practice of full, heavy work by day followed by daily evening school continued through college and they eventually graduated from commerce school - *Escuela de Comercio de Santiago de Cuba.*

Alfredo, who had an exceptional voice, was selected to be part of the commerce school choir. His dad, who did not approve of this, never attended any of the concerts.

One evening, twenty-one-year-old Alfredo, sitting at the dinner table with family, spoke up.

"I have been told that I have a good voice. The choir teacher sometimes asks me to perform a solo." With his forehead slightly tilted to the front, he raised his eyes to observe his dad's expression. America, Pucho and Pilar were in shock and scared awaiting to hear the father's reaction. Manuel's face remained inexpressive. Alfredo continued, "I'm considering pursuing a singing career."

At this point, Manuel reacted, "Absolutely not! Don't you see how many singers are starving to death! You will end up in one of those low-life night clubs, singing all night for a few *pesos.* You and your family will starve to death. Besides, we have built a reputation as a successful business family and now one of my sons will start singing in nightclubs. No way! That will be an embarrassment for the family."

"But Dad, I work here in the store with you, and I'm about to complete my commerce degree."

"Exactly, and you are thinking of throwing all that away for singing? Absolutely not! I don't want to hear any more about this." Without further discussion, Manuel got up from the table and left.

Silence.

Alfredo was devastated. His dream had been shattered once more. *Maybe someday in the future?* he thought.

12

WEDDING BELLS
Santiago de Cuba
1946

While attending commerce school in Santiago, Alfredo befriended his namesake, Alfredo Castañer, known as Gallego, who was studying accounting.

Twenty-six-year-old Gallego was easy on the eyes, tall and slim with a strong build, auburn hair, and stunning blue eyes. A year his junior, Alfredo, slightly shorter than Gallego, had jet-black hair and was of stronger build.

Both great-looking friends, each with their own style, were often noticed by the ladies but did not pay much attention to the flirting surrounding them since they were serious about their university goals and education.

Initially, Alfredo noticed Gallego's Spanish accent and asked, "Are you from Spain?"

"I was born near in Santiago de Cuba. However, my parents moved back to Spain, where they were from, with the idea of a better education for me and my siblings. We got entangled in the Spanish Civil War. What an experience! I'll tell you about it one day." At this, they struck up a friendship that grew over time. One evening, Alfredo asked, "Could I borrow that book you mentioned?"

"Of course, come over this evening, and I will lend it to you."

In the small colonial town of Santiago de Cuba, most houses were within walking distance from each other. His home was easy to identify.

"My house is right across from *Santa Lucia Catholic Church*."

That evening, after washing off the day's sweat and having dinner, Alfredo walked through the cobblestone narrow streets to arrive at the Castaner's home. At seven sharp, Alfredo knocked on the door of the unassuming residence. Bautista, Gallego's dad, opened the door, "Please, come in. My son told us you were stopping by tonight to pick up one of his books. Nice meeting you." Bautista said, extending his hand and signaling him to enter. "So, you are Manuel Barrio's youngest son from the furniture store. Please sit down." Bautista's Spanish accent was immediately noticeable.

"Yes, he is, Dad," responded Gallego as he entered the living room with the book in his hand. "Let me introduce you to my family. This is my dad, Bautista, who you already met, and this is my mom, Maria." The grey-hair fifty-five-year-old heavy-set, a typical-looking Spanish woman approached the living room wearing an apron and drying her hands with a kitchen cloth,

"Roman, Aurora, Enedina, come over to meet my friend from school," shouted Gallego. To Alfredo's surprise and delight, two beautiful young ladies entered the living room.

"How come you never told me that you had two beautiful sisters? Nice meeting you both," Alfredo said politely while slightly bowing his head and extending his hand. Although twenty-five-year-old Aurora was known as the most beautiful of the two sisters, the younger sister by two years,

Enedina, with her expressive blue eyes, immediately captured the guest's attention. Alfredo left home that evening with butterflies fluttering in his stomach. Her sparkling blue eyes continuously flashed in his mind as he could not seem to think of anything else. Through the evening conversation, he learned that she attended the town's all-girls institute.

The following afternoon, Alfredo hastily prepared himself and hurried from work toward the all-girl institute, eager to catch a glimpse of the students leaving their classes. On that particular day, he merely observed without taking any action, dedicating the time to formulating his strategy for the upcoming day. However, when the next day arrived, at the exact time and at the same street corner, he unexpectedly encountered her. "Oh, hi there! Do you recall me? I'm your brother's friend from the school, the one who visited your house to retrieve a book just two days ago." Enedina, who was walking home with her friend Rosita, was happily surprised, "Oh yes, I remember. And how come you are here?"

"I was working in the area delivering some merchandise, and coincidentally, I saw you walking this way. So, I decided to come over to greet you." Alfredo was not used to lying, so he averted his eyes subtly, attempting to avoid meeting her gaze. But then he smiled and asked, "Can I walk you home?"

Enedina agreed with a small movement forward of her head. The three walked together while Alfredo initiated a brief, timid conversation.

"I think he likes you," Rosita commented to Enedina the next day as they encountered each other in their classroom.

"Oh no! He likes my sister, and talking to me is his way of getting to her," responded Enedina, shifting the books she was carrying.

"Why do you think that?" Rosita inquired.

"Well, my sister is a lot prettier than me. She is the oldest one, about his age, and she is the most artistic and talented one, so everyone likes her best." She smiled at Rosita.

"Well, I'm not convinced of that," was Rosita's response.

During several days that month, Alfredo showed up at the same spot, as Enedina and her friend walked out of school. He always used the same excuse. "I was in the area for work. May I walk you home?"

A few days later, Enedina acknowledged that maybe Rosita's theory was the correct one. A month later, Alfredo encountered his friend Gallego in school. "Do you think your family will accept if I request to visit Enedina?" he asked, trying to be casual.

"Oh, Lord!" Gallego was in shock. "They will be very surprised." But he, too, responded with a smile. "I think they will be happily surprised, but let me ask, and I'll get back to you." The next day the response was affirmative. The family had accepted the request for the beginning of the courtship.

Eight months later, "*¡Tu no sabes en lo que te estas metiendo!* - You don't know what you are getting into! She is not easy. She is my sister and I love her, but beware she has a strong Spanish personality." Alfredo had confided to his friend before asking for Enedina's hand in marriage.

Bautista was best friends with Father Arteta, the pastor at *Santa Lucia Catholic Church*. Many evenings, the priest would cross the street to visit Bautista or vice versa. They talked mostly about their shared memories of Spain.

"Bautista, has Father Arteta tried to convert you? I know you are Catholic, but you only go to church to talk to your friend." A relative inquired one day.

"I go to church to talk to my friend and to drink the wine! He is a great friend. And do you know? They have the best wine!" Bautista smiled.

"Well, we drink it before it's blessed," he responded, laughing at the situation. Then he added, "Do you know that we talk about everything except religion? He never talks to me about religion. Strange but true. We spend long hours reminiscing about our common Spanish heritage. We consider our visits our oasis of the day and have relaxed conversations while drinking the amazing wine and smoking the best Cuban cigars," he signaled with his body language the pleasant circumstances of their gatherings, savoring the flavor of the remarkable Cuban cigar.

Every Christmas Eve, Father Arteta came to the Castañer family to help him roast a pig on a stick. In the Cuban tradition, the best part of Christmas Eve is the time spent celebrating with a beer in hand with friends surrounding the manually turned roasting pig.

When Alfredo asked Bautista for Enedina's hand in marriage his smiling response was, "Of course, we already have the priest and the church, and we only have to walk across the street."

In November of 1947, Alfredo and Enedina were married by the hand of Father Arteta in the *Church of Santa Lucia.*

Enedina walked the aisle looking stunning in the beautiful wedding dress with delicate lace across the bodice and rimming the bottom hem. She wore white gloves and a veil that matched the lace, all designed and sewn by her talented sister, Aurora. Her expressive blue eyes sparkled stronger than diamonds as she walked slowly to the tune of the wedding march toward her most handsome and radiant groom.

Figure 11. Enedina on her wedding day.

Figure 12. Enedina and Alfredo surrounded by friends and family, November
1947.

13

CREATING A DREAM LIFE DURING
THE DICTATORSHIP
Santiago de Cuba and
Havana, Cuba.
1948-1949

One evening in their poorly lit tiny bedroom, "Eni, I have been giving this idea a lot of thought, and the urge to move on is nudging my heart. I see a brighter future ahead of us, but not here." Alfredo said to his wife.

A few months after their wedding, Alfredo faced his wife with the news as he walked, like a gentle but caged wild animal, from one corner to the other side of the minuscule room. A few steps were enough to cover each corner of the room. He craved a certain freedom which he did not find in his present life. It was time for him to escape the life his family had designed for him and move into his own.

"The future that I envision for us and our family is not here. Having my own business in Havana is hounding me. I can't stop thinking about it," he said carefully coming to a standstill to look at his wife's facial expression.

"I know, you've mentioned it over and over. This is not news to me." Eni paused, before adding, "Change is not easy. Both of our families are here in Santiago de Cuba. But I can feel your thirst for the dream." The thought of the busy city of Havana, although scary, felt bright and exciting for the young couple in search of independence and their future.

A few months later, as Alfredo walked the rambunctious streets of Havana, feelings of fear and excitement for the unknown invaded his whole being. The dramatic contrast between the quiet colonial roads of Santiago de Cuba and the busy, rowdy, glittery streets of Havana stimulated him, and he excelled most when fueled by inspiration. So many changes were happening in Havana at this time. Carlos Prio Socarras had been elected president in 1948 after Fulgencio Batista who had served as the elected President of Cuba from 1940 to 1944.

The eight years under Grau and Prío, according to Charles Ameringer, were "Unique in Cuban history. They were a time of constitutional order and political freedom. They were not 'golden years' by any means, but in two elections (1944 and 1948), Cubans had the opportunity to express their desire for a rule of civil liberties, the primacy of Cuban culture, and the achievement of economic independence. If there were sharp contradictions in Cuban society under the Partido Auténticos (the governing party), the circumstances differed only in degree from the complexities and dynamics encountered in free societies everywhere."[17]

Prío, called *El Presidente Cordial* - The Cordial President, was committed to a rule marked by civility, primarily in its respect for freedom of expression. Several public-work projects and establishing a National Bank and Tribunal of Accounts count among his successes. However, violence among political factions and reports of theft and self-enrichment in the government ranks marred Prío's term. The Prío administration increasingly came to be perceived by the public as ineffectual in the face of violence and corruption, much as the Grau administration before it.

This was the Havana where Alfredo landed in late 1948, intending to build his dream life. He left his pregnant wife behind in Santiago de Cuba, in the care of her family, to travel to Havana with his brother-in-law, Roman, and his lifetime friend and now partner, Alejo Cabrera.

Enedina was eight months pregnant when her husband made the decision to leave his father's successful business, *La Muebleria Barrio* in Santiago de Cuba, and relocated to Havana to manifest his aspiration of owning his own business. Although Havana was amid great corruption, building and owning a profitable business was possible and on the rise. The economy was booming for assiduous businesspeople.

"As long as you don't get in the way of the politicians, bureaucrats, and powerful individuals, they will not interfere with you. They will allow you to build your own business and thrive discreetly in this society. Only you must be very, very careful not to step on their toes." This was how Alfredo described the situation at that moment.

It was a time of excessive contrasts with sectors of the nation in poverty and illiteracy versus excessive luxuries and pleasures amongst high-ranking government officials and mafia leaders. Amid those extremes, a middle class of hard-working individuals had been able to survive, and some, such as Alfredo and his partners, were emerging in this society. Working hard while staying under the radar was the key to thriving in business and taking advantage of the influx of money in Havana.

A pregnant Enedina stayed in Santiago de Cuba with her

family, waiting to give birth to their firstborn and allowing her newlywed husband to start his business and prepare their way for a new life in Havana. Alfredo, who was a proud young man, could have asked his now wealthy father, the one who worked himself up from his orphan stowaway origins, for monetary assistance. However, Alfredo settled for the route of independence.

The three partners lived for several months under the utmost restricted economic conditions. They would only eat once a day at a cheap nearby Chinese restaurant, and they would live in rooms that they set up temporarily in the same building they rented for their hardware business. One afternoon, after taking their meal orders, the Chinese waiter said, *"¡Tu todo lo pide con aló!* - You order everything with rice!"* They all laughed.

"Of course! *Arroz Frito* - fried rice, *Arroz con Leche* - rice pudding, that's the cheapest and most filling! We need to feed our hungry bellies with little money."

In the early afternoon of January 1949, twenty-three-year-old Enedina, with newborn Mary in her arms, boarded a train for the sixteen-hour trip from Santiago de Cuba to Havana.

"¡Mi hija, ten cuidado! - My daughter, be careful!"* warned Enedina's mother, Maria, as she saw her young daughter with her baby in her arms, boarding an old, corroded train, the only available method of transportation at that time. Maria could not deny her origins. The heavy accent and her European features easily gave away her roots, "Thank God Lucia is accompanying you. It's so dangerous and such a long trip! You are so young and with little Mary in your arms."

Enedina replied, trying to extinguish any doubts from her mom's worried mind. "I know Mom, but don't worry, I'm strong, I can do this. Besides, Lucia is accompanying me," Enedina's blue eyes flashed with excitement, "Alfredo is anxiously waiting for us. He is there by himself, fighting to build a future for us. I need to be by his side. Besides, there is security on board; we will be safe."

"Be careful and discreet when you breastfeed. Lucia, please take care of my granddaughter!" Turning to Lucia, "Thank you so much for keeping them company! Please, be safe!" She stopped to take a breath of hope and then continued, "And don't forget to send a telegram as soon as you arrive!"

In preparation for departure, the last whistle call of the train blew in the chilly winter afternoon.

"The train is departing. We must go! I love you, Mom!" Enedina announced while Maria extended her arms in an attempt to embrace both her daughter and the baby with one big hug. The young cousins ran to the door handle and up the stairs into the train. Once inside the cabin, they rushed to find their seats.

They found their seat numbers on top of two torn synthetic plastic train chairs where they landed, feeling much less comfortable than desired. Enedina's excitement did not allow her time to reflect on the lack of comfort that they felt during the sixteen-hour train ride. Indeed, a difficult night went by. The loud sound of the engine, the rough, cramped plastic-covered seats, the bumpy ride, and the baby in her arms made it just about impossible to get comfortable. However, exhaustion did eventually kick in and Enedina managed a few hours of sleep.

The next day, another cool January morning, the train finally approached the Havana train station. Enedina was filled with excitement at the expectation of seeing her newlywed, handsome husband.

Alfredo, a simple, practical man who lacked romantic skills, was also thrilled waiting for his beautiful bride and newborn daughter. During the last months, after long hours of daily work, he prepared a modest apartment on the second floor of the warehouse building located at the intersection of the streets Monte and Pila in Havana. He cleaned it, and with the little money that he had, he furnished and prepared his humble, tiny new home. The only furniture was an inexpensive wooden bed, a dresser, and a small used dining table with two chairs.

Early in the morning, with joy in his heart, he walked to the food store in the neighborhood, purchased some groceries for a few days, and returned to store them in the small old *Frigidaire* and single pantry shelf in the minuscule kitchen. Then, he washed up, combed his hair, put on some cologne, and headed out with excitement to welcome his new family. On his way to the train station, he saw a duster in a store window and realized that they needed one, so he bought the duster and continued on his way.

The train was just arriving, and Enedina was anxiously looking out the window and could not wait to see her husband. "Look, Lucia, there he is! And he is bringing me flowers!" Tears of joy rolled down her cheeks. As they disembarked, Alfredo anxiously pushed his way through the crowd. The slow motion of the crowd made the time seem eternal, but finally, they met, and the mutually awaited embrace finally arrived. Filled with elation, their embrace proved even more eternal.

"Let me see my baby," Alfredo said, but afraid of her fragility, he stepped back saying, "She is too little, and I have no experience carrying babies."

Finally, Enedina said, "Can I have my flowers?"

Alfredo, puzzled, responded, "Which flowers? Oh, you mean the duster? Oops!"

14

ROMAN AND OLGUITA
Havana, Cuba.
1949-1950

One of Alejo Cabrera's clients used to say, "The moment we see you walking in, we know that we will end up buying things that we never knew we needed. We don't know how you do it, but you always manage to do that." Alejo had the natural instincts of a salesman. He could make people believe that what they needed was precisely what he was selling.

The three partners, Alejo, Alfredo, and Roman, managed to create a strong, dynamic team. Each was passionate about their different but complementary roles with only one main goal in mind—success. Was it fate? Was it the combination of hard work and perseverance? Or was it the fact that these three people had their roots embedded in the stubborn and highly industrious culture of the Spaniards who emigrated to Cuba in the first half of the twentieth century?

Alfredo was the diligent and conscientious administrator who knew his inventory to the last smallest screw and was on top of his business down to the last detail. His vision was the driving force of the team.

Roman Castañer, Enedina's brother, Alfredo's brother-in-law, was the assiduous accountant who knew exactly how to balance and keep afloat the business' finances. A great team of harmonizing talents plus intense, consistent work was the combination of success for *Cabrera Barrio y Compañía*, the hardware store.

On a warm summer afternoon, Olga, a beautiful, voluptuous brunette who lived in the neighborhood of the recently opened hardware store, walked by on her way back from her job as a salesclerk at a woman's clothing store. As she stared through the window into the hardware store, she was captivated by the sight of this handsome man who was completely absorbed by his books. Filled with excitement, she continued on her way home, and upon her arrival, she commented to her sister Celia, "You have to see this hunk of a man! He works at a new hardware store that recently opened close by, just there." She pointed with her hand, "On the same corner of Monte and Pila. I walk by it almost every day, returning from work."

"Olga, but do you know if he is single?" replied Celia, intrigued by her sister's excitement. "But you don't know who this man is."

"No, I don't, but I intend to find out soon. You must see him. He is tall, handsome, strong, black hair, beautiful blue eyes." She went on and on as if she was under the spell of this fantasy man beyond her attainable dreams. Celia raised her eyebrows and then resumed her tasks.

The next morning, Olga took longer than usual to get dressed. Her make-up was slightly more dramatic than usual, and her dress was a summer-flowery silk-like fabric she knew would cling to her figure, enhancing her curves. A slightly revealing neckline was the perfect choice for the occasion.

As Celia observed her sister leaving for work, the obvious

question came up. "Where are you going? To work? Are you sure?"

She would not respond. Only the wink of her eye would hint at her plan for the day. On this hot but slightly breezy afternoon, Olga strolled up and down the dusty street, accentuating the movement of her hips and the movement of her eyes as she passed in front of the windows of the hardware store. Roman, being the serious, assiduous person that he was, did not lift his eyes from his accounting books. She left feeling a little discouraged but not defeated; tomorrow *will be another day, And another attempt!* She grinned at her lovely reflection in the window and returned home.

The strolling happened for several consecutive days without success. "I don't know what to do," Olga complained. "This guy never lifts his eyes from his work!" She commented to her sister at the end of the week, frustrated by her multiple failed attempts.

"I have an idea," Celia replied. "Just walk inside the store saying that you need to buy a screw, a hammer, anything, something! Start a conversation with him."

"A lady walking into a hardware store! Are you crazy?"

In 1949 it was not socially acceptable for ladies to walk into hardware stores.

"They will never believe me," she responded, twirling around with an attitude. "It will be too obvious! And besides, what would they think of me?" She shook her head in disapproval of her sister's suggestion.

"Do you want to meet this guy or not? If you continue rambling up and down the street, he will confuse you with a prostitute looking for work," her sister said.

"I know, I have already received suggestive gazes from other men on that street. And the one that I want has not even noticed me."

"You see, so you better stop doing that and find another way."

From the second floor, Enedina observed the provocatively dressed lady. *A fitted dress with those curves and dramatic make-up so early in the afternoon. Uhm! Who is that woman?* Seeing her ambling up and down the street in the afternoons, Enedina became suspicious of this intriguing woman. Enedina's nature was to suspect the worst of everyone, and she trusted very few. She knew that this woman was not like her, not like her sister, or not like her friends. *A decent woman does not dress provocatively and does not parade herself before men.* However, being aware that her views were rather provincial, she decided, at least for the moment, to give this exotic woman the benefit of the doubt.

Alfredo did not hear any of this from his wife since Enedina's philosophy was to never point out to her husband any seductive behaviors of other attractive women.

"Most men do not become aware of those things. However, if we point it out to our husbands, they will notice, and then, we wives may be in trouble." She would gossip with her friends about what she believed were her strategies.

That Thursday afternoon, there was a commotion in front of the store, "A woman tripped and fell on the street!" A passerby shouted. Soon, she was surrounded.

"Are you ok lady?" said one of the spectators approaching her.

"Let me help you." said another passerby.

"No, no, thank you! I just need some time," Olga replied, badly faking her pain. She was hopeful that the commotion would grab Roman's attention and that he would finally notice her.

Well, it took a while for him to realize what was happening. But he finally rushed outside to see what had disturbed his day. As he got to the site of the incident, Olga inhaled deeply and, trying to mask her pretense, said with a flirtatious voice, "I think I broke my ankle. Could you help me?"

Enedina, who also heard the commotion from the second floor, ran to the window. Seeing the mysterious woman on the street raised her suspicions of this audacious character even more.

"Watch out, that woman has been walking slowly along the streets, and I don't trust her intentions. Besides, she is not like us," Enedina scolded her brother that evening.

"You are always so mistrustful! The poor woman just fell!" Twenty-six-year-old Roman, who had been working intensively and without a girlfriend for some time, immediately disregarded his sister's comments. Roman was mesmerized by this woman from the first moment he laid eyes on her. He completely ignored the warning.

But this accident changed Roman's life forever. They married a year later. Roman and Olga fully enjoyed their romance. She never bore a child, but they just lived for one another. She called him Romy affectionately, and he took care of her to the extent of even cutting her steak at dinner time. "Romy, would you cut my meat for me?" she would purr.

In addition to working many long hours at his accounting

jobs, he would be enticed to do most of the housework upon his return home. Olga used to spend long hours looking at magazines and reading stories of royal families in other parts of the world while waiting for Romy to come home from work.

Women neighbors and family would watch and comment, "How is it that she manages to keep him so obsessed with her? She has not even given him a child, and she does very little as a housewife! Hmm."

15

NORA

AND THE HARROWING TRANSITION
Havana, Cuba.
1958

She walked in, standing straight with distinctive elegance and self-respect. Slim, beautiful, with a dark complexion, she wore medium-high heels and a perfectly pressed light-colored linen dress, looking as fresh as if she had just stepped out of the shower. On a humid fall morning in 1958, Nora walked into the newly built Barrio residence to be interviewed for a housekeeper position. She carried with her a special aura of respect, cleanliness, and gentleness.

"When she dresses up to go out on her days off, she looks like the queen of this house," Alfredo said with a smile on his face several months after hiring her. Nora would take pride in dressing up. Her hair was worn straight and elegantly twirled into a bun on top of her head. This would add a little height to the five-foot-two inches of her very petite figure.

Before 1959, most medium to high-income homes in Cuba were built with at least one room for service personnel, usually located close to the kitchen. Alfredo had finally achieved an economic position where he was able to provide his wife with help for the house. They had built the house of their dreams, and now they were hiring a housekeeper to do the cleaning, laundry, and light cooking. Thus far, Enedina had had a difficult life and her husband wanted to reward her for all she endured. She survived war and famine in her childhood and later lived in shaggy tiny apartments, working hard to take care of their home and daughters and to help her husband achieve his dreams of building his own business. Now, he was thrilled to provide her with a beautiful home and the help he felt she so much deserved.

Nine-year-old Mary and seven-year-old Gladys grew to appreciate and love Nora. Although she was occupied most of the time with household tasks, she would always find time to smile and be gentle with the girls. She kept her distance and respect, but her behavior was always sweet and kind. She knew what the girls liked, and she treated them to yummy snacks, mostly upon their arrival from school after a long and tiring day.

"*¡Que buena vida*! - What a good life!" Alfredo would tell Enedina with a smile of satisfaction when he saw her relaxing in her comfortable and charming home while all the tasks were being fulfilled with Nora's help.

"*Aprovechalo, porque no te va a durar*. - Enjoy it because it may not last forever."

Although he said it jokingly, later, he regretted saying it. Indeed, their dream lasted briefly, just a little over a year, when the tornado of communism swept through the island with destructive winds of social collapse.

By January 1, 1959, Cuba was under siege. A change in power took place when the Castro revolutionary coup removed the Fulgencio Batista dictatorship as he fled the country. Chaos reigned throughout the island, where thousands of people were detained, incarcerated, tortured, and killed for no other reason than a suspicion of being *Bastistianos* (those who were part of Batista's government) or anti-revolutionaries.

"They shot them! They shot them there on the street in front of my eyes, and for no reason, they were just partying! They were all so young! How could the government do that?" Their friend Mercedes shouted in anguish.

She had just witnessed, from her apartment window, the shooting of a group of young men who were only laughing and walking down the street. Blood splattered all over the sidewalk, people were running in a frenzy, and observers were in a panic. One of the young boys, who was shot in the arm, returned to help his fallen friends. Witnesses like Mercedes were traumatized by fear and confusion.

"They violated the curfew. It was past the curfew time," a neighbor replied as the two of them stayed safely inside.

"But they were heading home after a celebration. This is so senseless!" responded Mercedes in distress and frustration.

Shootings, tortures, and incarcerations were ubiquitous throughout the island. By the hundreds, people were taken to the *Paredones de Fusilamiento*. Innocent people lined-up in rows against a wall, with no proof of guilt or trials required, were shot to death and then thrown in mass graves. Some families whose members were missing never knew of their whereabouts.

Hopes were hard to extinguish, especially when they had been harvested for a long time. Although the fear spreading through the island should have opened the eyes of many to the reality of the new regime, people were still hopeful that the revolution would eventually bring a better life.

For the sake of the kids, the tradition of *El Dia De Los Reyes Magos* - The Three Kings Day, continued on January 6, 1959. Mary and Gladys woke up to see their two new living room curved sofas filled with Christmas presents. A sofa was assigned to each one of the girls. One big, beautiful doll sat on each sofa, and boxes with red bows, beautiful wrappings, games, and presents were all over. Nora observed the scene from a distance.

"Vengan a ver que les dejaron los Reyes - Come and see what The Three Kings left for you." Alfredo exclaimed, standing by Enedina's side in the living room, watching the sparkling eyes of their two daughters, who, like two little elves in their pajamas, were first peeking through the partially open door of their bedroom. But then, they ran out toward the spectacle of a room full of dazzling and glittering presents. Jumping, dancing, and screaming their joy with glowing faces.

"This is the doll that I wanted! Thank you, Three Kings!" exclaimed Gladys, holding on to a beautiful porcelain-faced doll.

"This is the game that I wanted!" exclaimed Mary.

"Did the Three Kings take the letter that we wrote? Did the camels eat the grass? Did the Kings drink the milk and eat the cookies that we baked?"

These questions were flowing out of the girls' mouths while ecstatically tearing apart wrapping paper in search of the next surprise. They jumped from one side of the sofa to the other side, not able to decide which packages to open first and which game to look at first. Gift paper and bows flew away as they opened each gift with elation. Everyone was enjoying the wonders of the moment.

"Come over, Nora, see my beautiful doll!" said Gladys. Her excitement was evident in her eyes as she showed off her doll. Nora embraced the girls, sharing the joy of this precious moment.

~ ~ ~

A few months later, that same year, the girls were flown away from the island, escaping the dangers of the political turmoil.

"¡*Latifundistas*! - Landowner bloodsuckers, all of you with a good economic situation are sucking the blood of the poor," were Castro's words on the radio.

Nora, like many other housekeepers, returned unwillingly to her humble hometown, somewhere in a low economic area of the island. Her hopes for progress were shattered. However, Nora met her future husband, and soon they were married. Enedina and Nora stayed in touch and continued their friendship. But less than a year after her marriage, tragedy occurred.

"Hello, this is Enedina. Am I speaking with Ester, Nora's mom?"

"¡*Ay mi'hija si supieras lo que ha pasado*! – Oh, my friend, if you only knew what happened," responded Nora's mom as she answered the phone.

"What happened?"

"*Mi Norita murio* - My little Nora died."

"No! What do you mean?" asked Enedina in disbelief, "How did this happen? I was calling to see how she was doing with the pregnancy and her first baby." Enedina could hear the crying and the lamentations.

"They could have saved her if they knew what they were

doing! She had complications from her pregnancy," Ester continued. "The new health system is chaotic, the good doctors have left the country, there are no medications, the hospitals are disorganized, it's a disaster!"

"I'm so sorry!" Enedina could not control her tears. "You know how much we loved her," she said with great grief in her soul, "I can't tell my girls now. They will be so sad!"

"Yes, I know. She loved you, and she loved the girls so much. You were always so good to her."

Enedina hung up the phone in desolation. "Our lives are collapsing, and now poor Nora is gone. One more aftershock has been added to the earthquake of our lives." Enedina said no more, crying in silence, *May she be rewarded in heaven for all the good deeds she did for us.*

16

JAMAICA

Kingston, Jamaica
1960 - 1961

On November 3, 1960, Alfredo and the girls gazed out the airplane window, reminiscing about the life left behind. They fretted at the unknown life ahead as they flew above the mysterious island the girls would call home for the next year. And it was to be.

"What am I doing? What will I do?" Alfredo moaned, absorbed in his thoughts.

Like many others, they boarded this flight in desperation to get as far away as possible from the imminent danger and political uncertainty of Cuba, their homeland. They were especially upset by the expected uprising, the fear that the communist government would implement radical measures akin to those previous experiences Eni had endured back in Spain twenty-four years prior.

They had lasting memories of bloody confrontations in Spain between Franco and the leftist government. Alfredo's mind, in turmoil, was wrapped in fear for their future and anger at the treason. The new government, which so many had supported, believing in the good intentions of the leaders, turned out to be a bloody communist dictatorship whose only goal was to destroy a flourishing country with its thirst for power. How could an alleged savior turn their homeland and their lives overnight into a living hell? Alfredo, fearful of the fate awaiting them, was going to fly his daughters out of hell into safety, away from the looming danger.

Twelve-year-old Mary and nine-year-old Gladys were anxiously bombarding their father with questions. "Dad, who is waiting for us at the airport? Where are we going? What if *Tío* - Uncle, is not there?"

"Tío Balbino will be there waiting for us. You will see your three cousins and will have the opportunity to play with them. How exciting!" Alfredo responded, attempting to stay calm for the sake of his daughters. He had prayed to God for guidance often and more in the last few days than in his whole life.

"Please, return to your seats," the voice of the pilot came on the speaker, "we will be landing soon at the *Kingston-Norman Manley International Airport* in Jamaica." The two girls gazed at each other and then at their father with shaky stomachs and fear on their faces.

As passengers disembarked, Mary and Gladys moved slower than most. Scared and holding on to their dad, they looked around this unfamiliar and unusual place. Everything felt different to them.

"Dad, I don't understand the signs. How do we know where to go? Where is our luggage?" They were faced with a language they could not understand and the features of people who were different from what they were used to seeing back home. The confusion was obvious as the three walked close together, hesitantly analyzing every sign, every stand, every person.

"Tío Balbino!" Finally, in the very small airport, they

spotted a familiar face. The sisters ran to hug him, "Tío, we are so glad to see you! This place is so bizarre!"

"Aurora had to stay home with the three kids," said Tío, "Let's get your luggage and go home."

The next day, as planned, Alfredo took a taxi with his daughters to a prestigious Catholic school in town. The plan was to leave the girls in boarding school until Castro was destitute and peace and democracy were re-established in Cuba.

"This should not take more than a year; this regime will not last," was the phrase overheard continuously by an increasingly larger group of the Cuban population.

A nun with a gentle demeanor invited them in. "Please come, the principal is expecting you." The girls walked shyly into a huge, intimidating office with a big, beautifully carved, varnished desk. A tall, overpowering, but placid Franciscan sister, seated at the desk, smiled welcoming them into her office.

The school, *The Immaculate Conception Academy*, was founded in 1858 by a group of Franciscan Sisters who came from Scotland to Kingston, Jamaica, to establish a boarding and day school for girls. Students from prominent Catholic residents in Jamaica, as well as from Latin America, Canada, and other countries, attended the school.

An air of compassion and willingness to assist the family during this time of distress was evident and prevailed throughout the meeting.

"Sister, I have no words to show my appreciation. You do not know what we are presently going through in our country. Fear, violence, death, injustice. The concern of having our daughters exposed to the risk is unbearable,"

Alfredo expressed in anguish with watery eyes.

"Go in peace, sir. We will take good care of your daughters."

Alfredo, trembling at the idea of separation, embraced his daughters. The compassionate nuns offered the family all the assistance required.

Although the school offered them love and shelter, the girls were distressed by the trauma of the sudden changes, especially that of leaving their parents.

"I'm scared, Mary. I know how good these nuns are, Dad told us, but these are strange people that we have never seen before. And I don't understand what they say," Gladys sobbed, her face in her hands.

The next morning, Mary scolded Gladys, "You wet your bed!"

"I'm sorry, I did not mean to," the younger sister responded anxiously.

The nun in charge of the rooms overhearing the commotion came around and lovingly responded, "I'm sure she didn't mean to. She is nervous. This situation is hard for her." And she gently took over the linen change.

The morning routine started with getting dressed, having breakfast, and heading to their next challenge, the classroom.

"Why is this teacher hitting me? Why am I placed every morning in this line to be punished?" Nine-year-old Gladys, with tears in her eyes, could not understand the meaning of this mean teacher's actions toward her, as well as toward a selected few of the students in her class. Every morning, Gladys, clueless of the motives, as she entered the classroom, was placed in a side row with several other kids in her class. The teacher, a heavy-set lay woman in her fifties

with an unfriendly face, comfortably seated at the teacher's desk, started her daily protocol.

Each student in the row, one by one, had to place their hand on the teacher's desk, and she would slap them with a ruler. In the 1960s, certain forms of corporal punishment were common practice in many countries, including in some states in the US.

That hurts! Gladys thought while her furrowed brows and reddened skin could not hide her sadness.

Being away from her parents for the first time in her life in a strange country, not even understanding the English language, and no one understanding her, was too much to bear. She couldn't help but have flashbacks of the days back in her country, in the beautiful school that she loved so much, which she had to forsake. She remembers the day that she overheard, "Catholic schools are closing all over the country." The Communist Party that took over the island closed churches, nationalized properties owned by religious organizations, and had forced the faithful underground.[18] The sweep was so broad in the 1960s that Fidel Castro even closed the Jesuit high school that he and his brother Raul had attended, forcing the priests to pack up and move to Miami. That was one of over 400 Catholic schools closed throughout the nation.[19]

Gladys daydreamed of the time when she was one of the top students in her class. She vividly recalled the blue-ribbon awards that she received at the end of every school year for her good grades and conduct. Now, all was a rude awakening, *And for what? I don't even know why that witch is spanking me!* She thought and felt miserable, sad, mistreated, isolated.

On the third day of consecutive punishments, she decided to find out why she was always selected for the torture line while many other kids were not. She turned to the girl next to her, begging her, and with a gesture, she asked, "Why is she hitting me?"

Although this girl did not understand a word she said, she was perceptive enough to say, "Homework! You need to do homework." Gladys had no idea that homework was being assigned. She could not understand a word. She did not even know the meaning of the word "homework", but she decided to follow her friend's clue.

At the end of class, when homework was assigned, her friend pointed out on the board where the teacher had written the page number of the book, and she copied them down. That evening, she ran back to her room in search of help.

Since this school is an international academy with students from many countries, I'm sure I can find someone who can help me. She thought, looking for a boarding student who spoke English and Spanish. That night, she did not rest until her homework was done.

The next day, as soon as she got to class, she proudly displayed her homework. Then, pompously, she walked directly to her desk, skipping the torture line. She landed on her chair, shaking her curly, dirty blonde ponytail and winking at her new friend with gratitude and satisfaction. *After all, I should have never been on that torture row.*

~ ~ ~

"Their parents send them here to keep them out of trouble," Mary whispered in Gladys' ear. Gladys was too young to understand some issues, and she was seldom interested in gossip. However, the older sister, maybe a street-wiser, had heard that some girls were sent to that school because they were in trouble back home.

"What! How do you know?"

"I overheard their conversations." By this time, Mary had learned enough English to understand some of the gossip. "One girl in the dorm," Mary whispered with a bewildering expression on her face, "this 14-year-old girl from another country was taking pictures of herself NAKED. With a Polaroid instant camera! To send to her boyfriend."

"Oh, my God!" Gladys exclaimed. Both girls' mouths hung open in astonishment. Mary kept whispering the story with expressions of horror on her face. Gladys, considering that she had contemplated becoming a nun in her previous school, could not fathom such stories. "She must be making this up. This could not possibly be true," Gladys murmured and kept walking.

One day, while waiting in the lunch line, Mary said, "Stop doing that. Why are you stumbling on top of me? Stop it!" Mary kept telling her sister, trying to lower her voice. A disturbance took place among the girls in the line when Gladys fainted and fell to the floor. Sister Mary Ann ran towards the group to investigate the commotion.

The next thing Gladys knew was that she was in her bedroom with a nun force-feeding her.

"No, I can't eat that! Ugh," she murmured, spitting the food out of her mouth.

The gentle but firm nun said, "I heard that you fainted because you are not eating enough. You have to eat."

"I can't. I hate this food. It's bad. Please don't make me eat it. I'm going to throw up."

After arguing and trying unsuccessfully to entice Gladys

to eat the food, the nun gave up and left.

Seven months had passed from the day they arrived at the school, when one morning, as they were walking to their classrooms, Mary came to talk to her sister. "Do you know that these nuns close the school in the summer, and they go north to a summer retreat?"

"What! So, what's going to happen to us? Tío Balbino and Tía Aurora moved to Puerto Rico. We don't know anyone here in Jamaica. We are on our own!"

"I don't know," Mary replied. "We need to write home and tell Mom and Dad. We are going to be left alone on the streets in this scary place."

May 10, 1961

Dear Mom and Dad,

Please pick us up! The school is closing in a few weeks, and we do not know what to do.

Please, come over. We are afraid. What will happen to us? Please.

We love you,

Mary and Gladys

Alfredo opened this letter and panicked. He had not been informed of the closing of the school. The Cuban government had implemented new travel restrictions. Approval to leave the country could take months, while within weeks, their daughters could be left with no place to stay.

17

ALL HOPE IS LOST

Havana, Cuba.
April 17, 1961

lfredo's voice erupted with emotion on that fateful April morning, "They've invaded!"

His attempt to modulate his tone was overshadowed by the surge of feelings. At that moment, Enedina being the sole confidant of his outburst was a precautionary measure against the ever-watchful walls, thinking, *How does one restrain the cadence of excitement when one's lungs feel on the brink of bursting?* The walls may have had ears, but his very being resonated with unrestrained joy. The chambers of his heart proved insufficient to contain the enormity of the day's events—the news he had yearned for, the anticipation he had clung to, had finally materialized.

It was the dawn of April 17, 1961, when Alfredo, as well as countless other Cubans, both inside and outside the island, burst into joy at the news. They spent hours anxiously waiting by the radio. He knew, they knew, they prayed. Something big was hatching. Regaining their island and the return of their stolen dreams.

"Eni, the invasion started! They have landed! They are landing right now in the Bay of Pigs!" Alfredo exclaimed, overwhelmed with exhilaration as he walked around the house, desperately looking for his wife to share the keenly desired news.

"Are you certain about this?" Enedina responded, her disbelief evident as she instinctively clasped her hands to her head, an expression of shock etched across her face, "Lower your voice, I beg you, they are going to arrest us!" she implored with a whisper, finding it difficult to digest the news. "Oh Lord, let's pray for those brave brigadiers." Her voice was a fervent plea. "They must succeed! Please help them. Help us recover our island."

Ninety miles away from the island, on the other side of the Straits of Florida, millions were celebrating. In Miami, you could hear the screams of elation and chanting, "*¡Regresamos a Cuba*! - We are returning to Cuba!"

Many had left the island during the first two years of Castro's takeover. Away from the oppressive government, exiles were overjoyed but trembling with fear for the assault brigade. They held back tears of happiness at the news. However, the exhilaration was short-lived and quickly turned to despair as the news from the island turned sour.

In April 1961, more than a thousand Cuban exiles stormed the beaches at the Bay of Pigs, Playa Girón on the southern coast of Cuba, intending to ignite an uprising that would overthrow Castro's communist government. President Eisenhower had authorized the CIA to conduct a covert operation to rid the island of the security danger that this new leader of Cuba represented for the US. The CIA formulated the plan, recruited Cuban exiles, and equipped and trained them, creating Assault Brigade 2506. However, the plan underwent several last-minute changes as the new President Kennedy was adamant that the hand of the US Government needed to remain hidden at all costs.

Late in the evening of April 16th, the air strike set to destroy the fleet of Cuban bombers was canceled by President Kennedy.

His words were: "Cancel the strike!"

The decision was so last-minute that the brigade pilots were sitting on the runway and taxied into position for takeoff when they were told to stand down.

On April 17th, the Bay of Pigs invasion began, but there was no air support for the invading brigade. Once ashore, they were met instantly by Cuban armed forces, who outnumbered them. The salvaged and undamaged Cuban planes that had survived the canceled first strike two days before the invasion were now flying overhead, wreaking mayhem on the Brigade.[20]

The invasion failed miserably, and the exiles soon found themselves outgunned, outmanned, outnumbered, and out planned by Castro's troops.

"The invasion has failed!" was the excruciating cry of Cubans craving the return of democracy to their island. "We have been betrayed!" they howled as a gray cloud of depression wrapped Cubans in every corner of the globe.

The Bay of Pigs invasion failure was the decisive factor that made many exiles realize that they were not returning to their country, at least not anytime soon.

One thousand one hundred and thirteen Brigade 2506 members ended up in Cuban prisons.

~ ~ ~

"Now we must leave the island forever! There is no more hope!" Enedina wept with inconsolable grief along with the millions suffering oppression inside the island.

"We'll never return!" said many, despairing. Intense

anguish rippled throughout the hundreds of thousands in exile.

Pieces of the puzzle that led to those tragic days remained buried in the minds of a selected few. Many conjectures surfaced about what happened. Many excuses. Some wondered, "Did Nikita Khrushchev threaten the US to stay out of Cuba?"

These were only speculations, and no one was willing to disclose the truth. A year later, through the Cuban Missile Crisis, the Soviet Union openly displayed its alternative plans for the island.[21]

The only completely real version was savagely taken away two years later into the deep, dark corners of death. The bullets that took President John F. Kennedy's life on that dreaded sunny and mild afternoon of November 22, 1963, carried with them the only real and complete version of the reasons that led to the events of that day. Decisions that changed lives forever for the worse. The lives and destinies of millions of Cubans and their descendants, whose futures depended on the success of that day, were irreversibly and forever forsaken.

18
SEE YOU IN HEAVEN
Santiago De Cuba, Cuba.
1961

Pilar broke the news to her brother on a hot and cloudy, gloomy morning, "Dad is dying. Doctors have given him only a few months to live."

"The day that Fidel proclaimed all business owners as *¡Latifundistas!* Manuel succumbed to such depression that he did not want to live any longer. It's all gone. Everything has been taken away from him. Losing everything he worked for all his life was unbearable for him," Pucho, Alfredo's oldest brother, remarked.

"This was more than enough reason to lose his appetite," continued Pilar, the younger of the Barrio siblings.

The evil voice of the dictator resonated in their minds, "*Los negociantes imperialistas le han chupado la sangre al pueblo* - The imperialist businessmen have sucked the blood out of the people." Words that psychologically destroyed Manuel as well as many others. They knew that, in contrast to the dictator's statement, Manuel had cared for his workers for many years and provided work and a way of living for many families. He was loved and admired by his employees as he always helped them and their families in every possible way with work, food, shelter, and money. His employees would always back him up; they looked up to him because he was a hard-working, caring man.

Not long after Castro announced the intervention of all private businesses, Manuel became sick. The family thought it was depression; later, he was diagnosed with stomach cancer and died in less than a year. Everyone speculated that the grief had been so overwhelming that he did not care to live anymore.

It was May of 1961 when Alfredo was facing the double challenge of staying by his loving father through his illness and death or returning to Jamaica to rescue his daughters. Requesting permission to leave the country was challenging enough. Cubans who left the country were labeled as traitors of the revolution and accordingly were forced to surrender all their possessions to the government, including businesses, if they had not already been intervened.

Homes, with all furniture, equipment, decorations, valuables, and jewelry, were stamped as national wealth and could not be taken out of the country. Only one suitcase, which was thoroughly scrutinized at the airport, was allowed at the time of departure. The plan was for Alfredo to get to his daughters on time while Enedina stayed behind, holding on a little longer to their possessions with the hope that a domestic revolt, with or without the help of the US would occur to remove the communist dictator from power.

No one could know how long acquiring exit permits would take. If the papers arrived before his father's death, he would not be able to be with his dad the last few weeks of his life, a man he loved so much. On the other hand, his young daughters were in a foreign country on their own, not knowing the next day's fate. Especially knowing that the language barrier was a main factor in the limited communication between the nuns and the parents.

"Dad, I know that you are not doing well, but little Mary and Gladys are by themselves in a foreign country living with a good family, but one we really don't know. You understand that I must go. Besides," he continued, "the government ghouls are following me. I am under surveillance by the Committee for the Defense of the Revolution, the CDR. Someone, deep inside the CDR committee but who does not want to see me hurt, advised me that I must leave the country. They know that I'm helping the contra-revolution with a radio station at my house. Dad, I must go." Alfredo said as he embraced his father.

The CDR had been established by Castro to keep track of people in their neighborhoods.

"Son, do what you must do. Don't worry about me, I will be ok," Manuel said. They embraced again, and Alfredo left. In the grey afternoon, Alfredo sat alone in his car crying. He had imagined being at his father's bedside, holding his hand as he drew his last breath. Now, that was not going to happen. Through his pain, though, he knew that his young daughters had their whole lives before them and needed his strength far more than his dying father, who after all was, himself, a strong man.

Driving away, he reasoned that the strength his father's lessons had given him was to be tested at this time. His memories would always be with him, and with the comfort of that knowledge, he faced the uncertain road ahead.

The permit to leave Cuba arrived prior to his father's death. Knowing that his main responsibility lay with his young daughters, thirty-nine-year-old Alfredo flew alone to Jamaica to reunite with the little ones and shelter them with a sense of security in the midst of the present uncertainty in his heart. He bore the pain of leaving his sick father, knowing he would never see him again.

Figure 13. The Barrio-Viel Family, 1954.

19

THE COWBOY

Santiago de Cuba, Cuba.
Kingston, Jamaica.
1961

Overnight and with little notice, the siblings were placed temporarily in the residence of a wealthy and gentle Jamaican family of British descent. Mary and Gladys suddenly found themselves being transferred from the school to this opulent house. A feeling of being tossed from one place to another, not fully understanding why, invaded their minds.

"Mary, do you know where we are going? What is happening? Where are they taking us? Why are Mom and Dad not here?" Ten-year-old Gladys struggled to hold back tears amid a complex blend of fear of the unknown and deep sadness. Mary, also clueless about their fate, only knew that the nuns had arranged to provide temporary shelter for them with a trusting Jamaican family. No reasons were given or details about the arrangements made. Maybe the language barrier blocked the transfer of information. The multiple recent changes in their lives were not conducive to too much questioning, reasoning, or speculation about the specific arrangements between nuns and this peculiar but loving Jamaican family.

As the girls fearfully entered the beautiful mansion, they

felt welcomed and at ease. Aayla, a thin, tall, refined, light-complected black lady, was smiling by the door next to her 15-year-old daughter, who was also slim and well-mannered. A mixture of Jamaican and British features was evident. Both were friendly, and they received the newly arrived small guests with caring demeanors.

The first evening with the family was enlivening, with a trip to the airport. The refined lady of the house and her children, 14-year-old Devon and 15-year-old Tianna, were all dressed to the nines, and the two new guests were driven by a chauffeur to the airport. Now that Mary and Gladys had finally mastered the English language, they were faced with the peculiar British accent, which made it challenging to comprehend. However, they could understand that their dad was arriving from a trip.

Memories of their arrival day in Jamaica, almost nine months prior, flooded their minds as they entered once again the small Kingston airport. The family stood by a huge glass window to look into the runway while passengers from other planes deplaned, walking down the stairs into the landing track. Suddenly, a small plane landed, and the family was excited, "He is arriving in that little plane." Tianna announced.

Hmm. It looks like a private plane, Mary thought. *It doesn't show the name of one of the big airlines.*

As the door of the very small plane opened, a tall and peculiar man, we could guess in his late 40s or early 50s, exited.

"He is wearing a cowboy hat and boots," Mary whispered in Gladys' ears, "and he looks very happy."

The cowboy looked toward the airport and gestured as

an important actor waving at his fans, and the family waved back excitedly.

What is this? Who is this guy? Why is he wearing a cowboy hat in Jamaica? Are there cowboys in Jamaica? The sisters thought, perplexed and confused by this weird scene.

The new arrival did not pay too much attention to the two new little people in the group. He was too absorbed in his happiness. The sisters were too young to figure out if he was drunk or just very happy.

<center>~~~</center>

One hot July evening at the wealthy Jamaican residence, Gladys noticed that Tianna was missing,

"Do you know where she hides?"

"When her parents leave, she jumps the fence to meet her boyfriend," replied Mary.

"What! How do you know? Oh Lord, I hope we do not get in trouble for this. I hope they don't think that we are in any way covering up for her."

"Well, I'm uncertain about who takes charge when the parents are away. However, if the responsibility falls on the servants to ensure she doesn't venture out, our presence here serves as a source of entertainment for them." Mary continued, "and it's easier for her to escape unnoticed."

Gladys placed her hands on her open mouth, turned around sharply, and walked to hide in her room.

The siblings lived with this family until their dad finally received his permit to leave the country.

Alfredo could not see the last days of his father and was not able to attend his dad's funeral. Enedina stayed behind for another year, trying to hold on to their new house, business, and possessions. After about a month and a half,

Alfredo showed up at the home of the hosting British family. He had no words to express his gratitude. Despite his limited language skills, the family understood how grateful he was. The sisters packed, said goodbye, and away they all went in search of new horizons.

Alfredo gave a lot of thought to planning their next steps. He had to select a place where he could make a living for his family in a Spanish-speaking environment, so language was the next decisive factor for the family. Castro's government did not allow citizens who left the country to bring any cash with them. So, the next day, with very limited resources, the family boarded a plane to their next destination.

20

PERSEVERANCE AND
RE-STARTING A LIFE
San Juan, Puerto Rico.
1961

Mary and Gladys were thrilled to be back on a turf similar to home. "Dad, look at the signs. They are all in Spanish. Hooray! We can understand everything. And people are speaking in Spanish. Do you know how long it has been since we heard our language?" This time, no one was waiting for them, but they could care less because they could understand, and it felt like home. They were not scared anymore. It felt familiar as if the nightmare was finally over for them.

It was late July 1961 when they arrived at the *Luis Munoz Marin National Airport* in San Juan, Puerto Rico.

"Please, don't get distracted. Stay close by. There are too many people here," Alfredo instructed the girls. Loud Latin music was heard in the halls, maybe a little confusing for them, but they could sense a feeling of comfort in this land.

"We need to take a taxi to Tía Aurora's house," their father said. This was the same aunt who had received them in Jamaica the prior year. The Rodriguez had relocated to Puerto Rico also in search of a future for their family.

Alfredo had agreed with the Rodriguez family to drop off the girls with them again, but only for a few weeks until he could raise enough funds to afford their own place. The sisters stayed with their relatives, and Alfredo rented a room in a *casa de huespedes de hombres* - a boarding house for men. A place where only immigrant men in a similar situation as Alfredo and who needed a temporary place to live, could rent low-cost rooms. To keep the cost down, guests had to take turns cooking and cleaning the house.

The next morning, Alfredo went out to look for a map and the Yellow Pages telephone book to search hardware stores nearby. He knew everything about running a hardware store and he was knowledgeable of the kind of inventory in these stores. So, off he went, walking, since he couldn't afford a taxi. He joyfully stopped at every hardware that he found on his way, no matter how small or large it was.

"My hard work back home and what I learned at *La Escuela de Comercio* in Santiago de Cuba is paying off now." His face glowed with satisfaction as he collapsed in a chair while speaking to one of the men back at the hostel. He was humbling announcing that he had become the hardware salesperson of one of the stores.

Exhausted but proud of his achievement in such a short time and full of hope, "Soon, I will be able to bring my wife Enedina from Cuba, and I will rent a place to reunite my family," he said with confidence while showing through his demeanor, his urgency.

Every day, he woke up earlier than anyone else and went out with his briefcase. Dressed as professionally as he could and with the few pieces of clothing that he was allowed to bring from Cuba. What interfered with his goal was the discomfort in his feet. They hurt at the end of each long day after walking several miles and visiting store after store after store after store after store. He never gave up.

One day, he felt a burning sensation between his thighs, and not knowing what it was, he kept walking, visiting stores, and selling as much as he could. When he got home, he found his thighs were bleeding from the heat and the constant rubbing.

I can't rest. I need to treat myself today so that I can continue tomorrow. Using a first aid kit available in the hostel, he treated his wounds the best he could. The next day, he wrapped his inner thighs with gauze, and off he went again.

"What a great country! Anyone who works hard can shine and excel here." Alfredo would exclaim proudly to his Puerto Rican co-workers and clients. Although it required hard work, this new country was a great place to start again. And so, he did. In a few months, Alfredo was able to build a clientele and raise the money needed to reunite the family.

One Sunday morning, Alfredo picked up the girls from Tía Aurora's home, where the girls were living temporarily.

"Dad, where are we going?"

"You will see," Alfredo responded with a smile on his face.

As they parked, they entered a strange, huge building.

"Dad, what are you plotting? What is this place?"

Alfredo kept smiling, not saying a word.

"Darlington," Mary said, noticing the sign with the name of the building. They took the elevator to the ninth floor, and as they came out of the elevator, Alfredo pulled a set of keys from his pocket.

The girls seemed confused. As he opened the door, a small, almost empty apartment was evident, a tiny one-bedroom studio. Then, with his hand and a smile on his face, he showed the girls in, announcing, "Ta, da! This is our new home!"

"Dad!" The girls exclaimed with excitement.

"Dad, this is the most beautiful place ever!" The girls said, their faces glowing while tears of happiness welled up in their eyes.

"This is not the beautiful home we lost in Cuba, but this is our home now," Alfredo said with sadness in his voice.

"Dad, we are so happy. This is what we wanted. This is perfect, together again!" Gladys said, giving him a big hug. "Being together here is better than living or owning a castle anywhere in the world!"

It did not matter how small. It did not matter that it had no furniture. This was home—the place they had longed for all this time.

Home is where the love of our reunited family can thrive once again, Alfredo thought.

"Are these our beds?" Mary asked.

"Yes, these small bunk beds are yours. This is all I could afford," he replied gloomily.

"Dad, we love it! It's beautiful. Thank you, Dad!"

"And Mom? Is she coming?"

"The room is for your mom and me whenever your mom receives the permit to come," Alfredo replied, avoiding the question for now and focusing on their new project. "I'm trying to get a small used table with four chairs for us to have our dinners together again." Alfredo embraced his daughters and celebrated the significance of this moment in their lives. Their first home in exile.

~ ~ ~

Two weeks later, he informed Aurora over the phone, "I'm picking up the girls this afternoon. I have a surprise."

"Let's go," Alfredo said to the girls as he arrived to pick them up.

"Where are you taking us, Dad?" Mary inquired.

"You will see!" He said, trying to control his feelings.

They arrived at the airport and walked down the aisle to the waiting area.

"Dad, who are we picking up? Rober? One of our cousins?" They knew that all their cousins were these days trying to leave Cuba to avoid military service. Their dad would not answer their questions, but there was a glow in his eyes.

They waited and waited, and waited until the girls became impatient.

"I think we arrived too early," Alfredo told the girls while looking at his watch.

But suddenly, their eyes opened as they spotted what they considered the most beautiful woman in the world walking toward them. She sparkled! Her beautiful blue eyes filled with tears of emotion. They could not believe their eyes. This was a moment that would remain in their minds until the day they died.

"Mami, Mami, Mami!" Here, walking towards them, was the mother that they had not seen for almost two years! The girls ran to embrace her. For so long, they had anxiously awaited the moment that was finally here, *now!*

"Dad, you didn't tell us that Mom was finally coming!" The girls jumped up and down in joy, embracing their mom and kissing her all over her face. Enedina dropped her purse and carried on as the four of them suddenly became a never-ending carousel of tears, laughter, and joy.

The Darlington apartment was tiny, but the love and joy of reuniting the family were far greater than the limits of the universe. All the fortune in the world could not compare with the happiness felt by the family when, at last, they found themselves under the same roof together again.

21

OMERO
Cuba
1963-1980

"Requisa!" was the dreaded shout echoing through the halls of the filthy, decrepit prison at any unexpected time, mostly at night.

While the Barrio Castañer family was building a new life outside of Cuba, Omero, an acquaintance of the family was fighting with other brave men for the freedom of their country.

"The uproar, guard boots rushing through the halls of the overcrowded, murky, and dilapidated prison. Machetes, nightsticks, truncheons, wood batons, and clubs were hitting prisoner hands on the bars of the cells as guardsmen rushed down the prison halls shouting, "¡*Requisa* – requisition. *Requisa, requisa!*"

Inmates got on their feet instantly, in whatever little clothing they wore due to the excessive heat at the time, and embraced themselves with the courage to resist the physical torment that was coming their way. They were trained to immediately get in line and walk out one by one under the torture of the strenuous assault of the guards.

The guards formed a tunnel with their machetes and truncheons; their hands hit each passerby with all their might. Broken bones and bloody skins were the result as each inmate exited the dreaded tunnel of terror.

They braced for the pain, the humiliation, the degradation. Their only goal was to fight for their principles and for the freedom and liberation of their country. They did not fear death; they knew death was imminent, but the National Anthem stanza *Morir por la Patria es Vivir* - To die for your country is to live, was their motto.

On April 20, 1963, a group of contra-revolutionaries fighting to recover Cuba from Castro's recently declared communism and bloody tyranny were caught in the town of Bejucal in the Havana province. Omero and others, who were also part of the captured guerrilla group, were able to escape. Four of the escapees were shot and killed on the spot. Omero, a courageous, strong nineteen-year-old man at the time, who was the son of an ex-rural guard of the armed forces of the former president Fulgencio Batista's government, was able to escape along with others into the mountains.

For three days, he hid in a hole in the ground with four other rebels. On day three, they walked out slowly, one by one, fearfully, looking around and searching for hazards but perplexed. They were ecstatic to be stroked by the desired, but now unfamiliar, sunshine, which impacted their closed retinas in a painful but welcomed way. Each one went their own way.

Omero's father, hearing through his undercover contacts about the whereabouts of his son, arranged for him to hide at a sister's home, where he sought refuge for several months.

Then, on a hot morning in June, Omero decided to venture out of hiding and into the closest town. However, while in town, he was recognized by members of Castro's militia and was captured and imprisoned. All the ones who escaped with Omero were eventually caught and thrown back in jail, except Juan, who was never caught. He spent his life hiding on the island.

After being detained, Omero was transferred to the dreaded *Fortaleza de San Carlos de la Cabaña* – The Fort of Saint Charles, known as *La Cabaña*, an eighteenth century fortress complex located on the elevated eastern side of the harbor entrance in La Habana.

Che Guevara used the fortress as a headquarters and military prison for several years. During his five-month tenure (January 2 through June 12, 1959), Guevara oversaw the revolutionary tribunals and executions of suspected war criminals, political prisoners, and former members of the *Buró de Represión de Actividades Comunistas* - Bureau of Repression of Communist Activities.

Batista's entire secret police were massacred or disappeared. After Che Guevara's term in that post, *La Cabaña* continued as a dreaded political prison for Castro's political enemies. Prisoners were taken there for initial questioning and torture, and then transferred to other prisons on the island.

Omero's trial, whose outcome was determined before it started, lasted less than thirty minutes. He was condemned to twenty years in prison and was thrown in the area of *La Cabaña* named Galera 14. The testimony of an undercover snitch was taken as sole proof that Omero was indeed one of the rebels.

Omero spent two months in *La Cabaña*, and after being questioned in a trumped-up trial and suffering numerous cruelties his broken body was thrown in the filthy dungeons to rot. The odor of urine and rotting flesh invaded the overcrowded cells. Cockroaches and rats crawled in and out of the walls. The ill-treatment debilitated his body but not his spirit. His ideals of freedom, justice, and liberty strengthened him as well as those of other courageous inmates.

"Nongo Puig executed today!" The names of the prisoners who were shot by the firing squad in *La Cabaña* were announced daily.

"Eufemio Fernandez, attorney, executed!"

"Commander Humberto Sori Marin, executed!"

"Commander William Morgan, the American, executed today by the firing squad!"

"Commander Jesus Carrera, executed."

Commander was the highest-ranking position that anyone could attain in the government.

"He was brave! He was one of the few who dared to face and challenge Che Guevara." One of the inmates exclaimed,

"Mingo Trova! Son of the famous Guanabacoa's Regil coffee, executed!"

"Francisco, the American CIA agent executed today!"

Memories of the past recent executions were in the minds of the prisoners.

Jesus Sosa Blanco was arrested on February 16, 1959, and charged with having committed murders for Batista. His show trial was in the *Havana Sports Palace* before 17,000 spectators, and in the circus/ televised trial on February 18th, he was found guilty and executed.

They also knew that on August 30, 1962, four hundred and seventy-two men were sent to the *Paredon de Fusilamiento* – firing squad and were shot to death under the charge of conspiracy.

On May 9, 1964, Omero was among one hundred and nine inmates who were transferred from *La Cabaña* by a Russian aircraft to another concentration camp. It was time to make room for the newly captured rebels who were arriving daily at *La Cabaña* for new questioning and more torture.

These groups of prisoners controlled their eyes as they boarded the plane when they were suddenly riveted by the stunning, blue-eyed Russian woman piloting the plane. Of course, surrounded by a squad of guards, no one would dare give her a second look. They all gazed down but still caught glimpses through the corner of their eyes.

There were no seats inside the aircraft; prisoners were tied up in groups of two, and some traveled seated on the floor. The one hundred and nine prisoners were transported to their new incarceration destination.

Thirty miles off the southern coast of Cuba lies what was then known as Isla de Pinos. It is now known as *La Isla de la Juventud* - Isle of Youth, a beautiful 850 sq mile island, 31 miles south of Cuba, across the Gulf of Batabanó. The island, covered in lush vegetation and pine forests, lies almost directly south of Havana and Pinar del Río, and is not part of any province. Half of the island falls under a "special municipality" designation, which is administered directly by the central government. This classification prevents access except for those who have the proper permit from the Cuban government.

Since 1928, the Isle of Youth had been home to a dreaded model prison. The prison consists of five monstrous circular buildings, six stories in each one. Each circular building with a panopticon design allows the visibility of all prisoners. Towers in the courtyard of each one housed the sentinel guards equipped with machine guns.

By 1961, due to the overcrowded conditions, there were up to 4000 prisoners at one time, it was the site of various riots and hunger strikes, especially just before the Bay of Pigs invasion, when orders were given to line the tunnels underneath the entire prison with several tons of TNT.[22][23]

In the late 1960s and in the 1970s, the Isle of Youth served as "re-education camps" for thousands of Cuban homosexuals who were fired, detained, imprisoned, tortured, mistreated, and brainwashed.

As the plane landed, prisoners, tied in pairs of two, were instructed through heavy shouting to jump out through the back of the aircraft. The plane didn't stop its engines to unload the prisoners. Omero was tied to Oswaldo Camara, a *repentista*, a Cuban music folklore poet.

They were expected to jump out of the plane and immediately run and leap onto the truck that was waiting to transport them. The guards, as if they were cutting sugar cane, carried their truncheons with all their strength to strike down anyone who fell to the ground and did not jump immediately on the truck.

"*¡Parate, coño!* - Get up, dammit!" was heard over and over by the inmates as their partners fell. They knew they would be struck if they didn't jump up immediately.

After passing through the tunnel of terror and the welcoming reception, they were struck repeatedly by the guards, even as they walked toward the building. Once inside and directed to a dirty pavilion for fingerprinting, the jailers took hair samples, one from each side of the head. At the time, the prisoners were ignorant about why the guards took these samples. Later, they learned about the existence of a DNA catalog.

They were forced one by one to put on the same white shirt displaying each prisoner's number.

33508 – was Omero's number.

The height and weight of the prisoners were taken, recorded, and used to classify them accordingly.

Group 1 included doctors, intellectuals, students, and community leaders.

Group 2, farmers mostly of the *Second National Front of Escambray* - an independent guerilla group led by Eloy Gutiérrez Menoyo, Dr. Armando Fleites, and included others in the Cuban central Escambray Mountains. William Alexander Morgan "The American" was also a part of the Escambray group. While initially, the group supported Fidel Castro in his efforts to overthrow Cuban dictator Fulgencio Batista, after Castro took power, some of its members joined former Batista soldiers and local farmers in the Escambray Rebellion (1959-1965) opposing Castro.

Group 3, former Batista militias, and

Group 4 included everyone else.

The Camilo Cienfuegos' initiative of forced labor placed Omero in the Columbus marble quarry where he was forced to cut rock eight hours a day under the scorching sun.

"Collapsing of the inmates from de-hydration was common but immediately remedied with threats," Omero described. "We were always surrounded by guards, and anyone who would dare to move was shot to death on the spot." He continued, "The nasty and limited meals were insufficient to keep the energy for such forced labor days. In the morning, we were fed a piece of bread and hot water with sugar. In the evenings, we'd get either a nasty bowl of fish soup or cheap pasta, rice, or *boniato* – sweet potato. We were served Russian meat, which tasted like hell, or sardines, which were the only protein that we would get for the day."

"In the evenings, we were expected to take a shower with greenish, mold-smelly water. Our forced-labor duties were continuously changed, and inmates rotated so that we could not have a chance to talk or plan a breakout."

"Get out! All of you! We are moving you to another jail." Guards with wooden clubs in hand struck everyone to discipline them and showed that they were ready to kill anyone who would resist their demands.

Without prior notification, the prisoners were loaded into a truck and sent away to *Sandino* in Pinar de Rio, another concentration camp in the western part of the island.

Sandino was founded in 1964 as an artificial prison camp where the government forcibly removed peasant families from their homeland in the central Cuban Escambray Mountains. These peasants actually or supposedly supported the rebels in the fight against Fidel Castro's authoritarian rule in the civil war that flared up after the revolution from 1960 onwards. The buildings on site, which were fenced off with barbed wire for a long time, were built using forced labor by men abducted from the conflict zone in the province of Las Villas. After the construction work was completed, these men were able to bring their families, who had previously been separated from them, to live in these apartments under a permanent state of surveillance.

"Eighteen months later, we were moved again to *Melena 2*, in Melena del Sur. Another prisoner camp in the southern province of Havana." Omero continued describing the constant movement of inmates from one prison to another. In this prison, Omero met an inmate by the name of Rigoberto Fernandez Ponce, who became his very good friend and later his partner in business.

"Have you noticed that every day, close to 8:00 pm the electricity is disconnected for one hour?" Bencomo mentioned to Omero on a stifling summer afternoon after returning from forced labor. They were resting on a low cement wall in the courtyard of the prisoners' camp.

"I heard they do it to save energy," Omero answered. The courtyard was filled with prisoners and guards with guns on hand, always ready to shoot at the slightest movement or argument. Bencomo knew that Omero was unafraid and anxious to escape. And Bencomo was the perfect collaborator to consummate his plan. Without revealing anything with his facial expressions or body language, Bencomo walked slowly back and forth in front of Omero striving to disguise his internal turmoil.

"What's the plan?" Omero responded, looking out at the open space and barely moving his mouth or changing his facial expression.

"Tomorrow, 8:00 pm sharp! By the fence!" Bencomo replied, signaling by directing his eyesight to the exact spot.

"How do we ensure that we don't get shot like Alfredo Carrion?"

"His escape was in daylight, we'll be in the dark, no electricity, no alarms. And besides, the moon is on our side."

When the lights were disconnected, guards would walk between two parallel fences. However, Bencomo, Omero and three others did not give them time. They crawled up one fence like raccoons, then down, then up the next fence, like a flash at the speed of sound: no noise whatsoever and landing, one by one, on the soil on the other side. Omero's big blue eyes sparkled with excitement, illuminating the way through the dense darkness of the night.

This day good fortune was on their side; everything happened exactly as planned. Omero was twenty-three years old when, with five other inmates, all were miraculously able to successfully escape. The dry leaves crackling under their feet were almost too loud to bear as they slithered like snakes over the ground, and then ran low, quietly, looking back while moving forward as fast as possible.

Silence.

"No one has heard! Let's spread out!"

"Good luck!"

These were the last words of the five prisoners as they disappeared into the shadows of the mountains in the darkness of night.

Omero remained in hiding in the mountains for two and a half years. "My sister learned of my whereabouts, visited me, and brought me supplies. Some *guajiros* – farmers, who lived in the area also helped me and provided food." He described his means of survival while hiding. "During this time, I dreamt of one day eventually arriving in Miami, the land of hope."

The dream of so many Cubans, especially those in prison and those who fought for freedom.

The news came in that other prisoners escaped and were roaming the area. Searching quietly while keeping a low profile, Omero was able to find a way to make contact with them.

"They are planning a way out of Cuba into the dreamland! They have made contact to leave the island." He exclaimed in joy.

However, when his hopes were at their highest point, he heard a group of strangers walking with guns toward his hiding place. "We caught you, *gusano* - worm!"

He ran for his life in desperation, but they yelled after him, "*Parate, no te muevas que te matamos.* - Stop, don't move, or we'll kill you!"

One of the supposedly escaped prisoners was a snitch for the state security and had given them all away.

Handcuffed, he was taken to the police station in San Antonio de la Vega where he was interrogated with ghastly repression. Agents from the G2, the state security, came to transfer him to *El Castillo del Principe*, an eighteenth century fortress notable for its incredible architectural beauty and partially vaulted tunnel, which allowed protected movement about the castle, in addition to its large defensive ditches.

To Omero and the political prisoners, it was an old dungeon where he had to endure gruesome mistreatment for another year. He was sentenced to an additional three years of imprisonment, which was added to the original sixteen years of the earlier prison sentence.

On November 14, 1979, US President Jimmy Carter negotiated the release of 2500 political prisoners. And on March 3, 1980, Omero was able to board a flight to Miami.

The Episcopal Church of New Orleans, through the efforts of Leopoldo Frades, former bishop of Honduras, and later bishop of the Episcopal Church of Southeast Florida, raised $10,000 to sponsor this flight and the expenses for twenty-nine of the prisoners with selective family members.

Omero was miraculously selected for this flight and was one of 29 prisoners on board. After numerous years of struggles, incarcerations, and torture, his dream of arriving in the land of freedom finally was becoming a reality.

The efforts of one compassionate US president and the charitable hand of the Episcopal Church and his astounding bishop, created the miracle, rewarding these courageous men with the land of their dreams.

22

STRUGGLES AND SUCCESSES

Puerto Rico
1962

After years of relentless work in exile, one sweltering afternoon as Alfredo entered the headquarters of a renowned paint company to showcase his merchandise, he received unexpected news. Walking into the building with briefcase in hand, he encountered a distinguished gentleman in his late fifties with streaks of silver hair, who greeted him with a smile.

"I've heard that you are an excellent businessman," he said, extending his hand. "I am Francisco Cardona, Chief Executive Officer (CEO) of Glidden Enterprises for Latin America."

Surprised by the stranger's praise, Alfredo jokingly responded, "Who spread these rumors about me?"

Francisco chuckled and replied, "I have a reliable source. It seems you have experience in building and managing successful businesses from scratch. This information comes from a very reliable source." looking around and smiling at his employee seated at the nearest desk, acknowledging the fact that he knew what was coming next. "I have an interesting proposition for you, and I hope you consider my offer." Curiosity sparked within Alfredo as he listened to the

CEO.

"We have a branch of this company in the southern coastal region of the island, in Ponce, that is in desperate need of a skilled administrator. We believe that the branch has immense potential, but it lacks effective management. We are prepared to make you a generous offer that will also benefit your family." Mr. Cardona enticed, "As part of the package, we can offer your family the membership to the prestigious Ponce Yacht Club."

Alfredo's father, Manuel, a hardworking Spaniard, had instilled in him the values of skepticism towards easy opportunities and the importance of hard work for success. He remembered his father's words, *"Nada se logra de gratis en esta vida. ¡Si quieres triunfar, hay que trabajar muy duro!* - Nothing is achieved for free in this life, and if you want to succeed, you must work very hard."

With these teachings in mind, Alfredo felt hesitant and doubtful despite his excitement for the offer. He asked Mr. Cardona for more details about his role, the company's expectations, and its vision.

That night, as Alfredo returned home, joy and excitement filled his heart. However, he could not ignore the tumultuous life his wife, Eni, had endured, marked by wars, migrations, and exiles. Eni had experienced instability, multiple relocations, and the loss of possessions throughout her life. These memories of displacement and hardship weighed heavily on Alfredo's mind. Despite his excitement, he felt caught in a dilemma. Relocating and facing uncertainty again would require finding the right words to ask Eni to embark on this new journey.

Walking into the kitchen where Eni was preparing

dinner, Alfredo approached her and playfully tickled her side. "Eni, I have great news."

Eni turned around, her expression a mix of concern and hesitant joy. "I'm afraid to ask. What is this great news?"

"I received an incredible offer," Alfredo exclaimed. "Glidden Enterprises has made me an offer that more than triples my current salary! It's a dream come true!"

Enedina, cautious by nature due to the challenges she had faced in life, responded, "Remember what we've learned: if it's too good to be true, it may be fishy. Who made this offer?"

"Eni, it's a reputable company. The CEO of Latin America Operations personally made me the offer after hearing about the successful enterprise I built. Rolando, the man I deal with for sales, spoke highly of me. He suggested I could save one of their struggling stores from bankruptcy." Alfredo paused, studying Eni's expression.

"The challenge is that we need to move from San Juan to Ponce," Alfredo cautiously revealed.

"They say that Ponce is beautiful!" Cautiously he introduced joyful ideas with excitement in his voice as he continued. "Ponce is known as *La Ciudad Señorial* – The Majestic City, of Puerto Rico. They have great schools and the famous *Ponce Museum*. Many aristocratic families live in that city, including the Ferrer family."

Eni, worried but intrigued, bombarded Alfredo with questions, envisioning all possible negative outcomes. She had experienced more changes and traumas in her life than most could fathom. That night, they engaged in a lengthy conversation. Alfredo patiently addressed all her concerns until he finally heard the words he had hoped for.

"Okay," she said, her voice filled with a mix of apprehension and determination. "Let's do it."

Three weeks later, the family embarked on their journey to Ponce. Mary and Gladys were fourteen and twelve, respectively. They settled in a small but charming house rented with the assistance of the company's realtor program. The girls enrolled in a semi-private school run by North American nuns. For the first time, they attended a mixed-gender school where classes were conducted in English, providing a fresh experience compared to their previous all-girl school. Mary, the more spirited of the two, embraced this change wholeheartedly.

"The strict rules of the previous all-girl school run by European nuns suffocated me," she declared. "This new school feels more liberal, and the presence of boys makes it even more exciting."

Unfortunately, Mary's enjoyment of this new school was short-lived, lasting less than a year.

23

TUNNEL OF HOPE
THE ARRIVAL OF THE IMMEDIATE FAMILY
Ponce, Puerto Rico.
1962-1963

In the midst of their new life in Ponce, Puerto Rico, an unforeseen call disrupted the tranquility. Alfredo's brother Pucho reached out with an urgent plea, casting light on a dire situation that required immediate attention.

"Brother, Dora and I are deeply worried about our children's future. We must act now." Pucho shared his distress, "Would you let our two older kids stay with you for a few months in Puerto Rico? We need time to prepare for our departure from Cuba." The call arrived one tropical evening, as the sun painted the sky in a tapestry of colors. Pucho continued, "Manolo is nearing the age where he will be conscripted into the military. We've held on, hoping for change in Cuba, but it's only deteriorating. The militia service is perilous and abhorred by all. He will resist."

During the 1960s, the Cuban government conscripted between 250,000 to 300,000 men and women—not counting militia—in its standing armed forces.[24] The Cuban obligatory military service consisted of three years of unpaid slave-like labor.[25] This severity had grown in response to fears of a US invasion.[26]

Alfredo listened in silence as Pucho unfolded the

126

ominous circumstances. "Dorita, our daughter, is approaching the age of forced labor in the sugar cane fields, *A cortar caña* – off to cut sugar cane, in a world of hardship and exploitation.[27] We have requested the permits needed to leave the island, but the bureaucratic process is slow and uncertain. We're arranging temporary visas for Dorita and Manolo, disguising their departures as a visit."

Alfredo, despite the shock, couldn't refuse his brother's plea. "I understand, my brother. I will help you in any way I can." He pondered the challenges, "But getting them out safely won't be easy with the suspicions of the authorities."

Aware of his limited resources, both financial and inadequate space at home, Alfredo discussed the situation with his wife, "Eni, I have to help my brother and those kids. That's more important now than anything else."

"Well, we have no choice. God will provide!" Eni reassured him. "I always knew that since we were the first ones in exile, we would be the tunnel for the rest of the family. This is only the beginning of our family journey. We are their only hope."

~~~

In April 1962, Dorita and Manolito arrived at the *Muñoz Marin International Airport* in San Juan Puerto Rico. "Eni, let's head to the airport to pick up our niece and nephew. We do not all fit in 'my Cadillac,' but we will make it work." Alfredo smiled proudly about his 'Cadillac' - a 1950s Volkswagen Beetle car that he was able to buy after overcoming his financial struggles. Weeks after the relatives' arrival, one of the neighbors who loved to watch the family of six squeeze into the car said, "I don't know how you do it! Six big people inside that tiny Volkswagen!" The
~~~

neighbor would jokingly tease Alfredo.

Dorita's initial memory of the renowned Piquiña mountain remains etched in her mind, as well as an indelible first encounter with a sprawling network of roads that traverses Puerto Rico from west to east through the central mountain range—not a drive for the faint of heart. It is a two-lane road that crests steep mountains with farms on either side, skirts, sheer cliff drops, and hairpin turns. Horse-drawn carriages, big trucks, and nimble locals in their cars intertwine their paths as they traverse these roads.[28] It was a scary adventure following the unsettling departure from Cuba within the confines of a diminutive Volkswagen Beetle carrying six sizable individuals.

As they settled into the household of their *tíos* - uncles, and *primos* – cousins, the reality of the small living space was overlooked in favor of the joy of being reunited. Eni had prepared two cots to provide beds for the recent arrivals. Dorita's cot was placed in the girls' room, already overcrowded. Manolito's was placed in a corner of the house near the living room area. The four cousins were as joyful as a chorus of laughing clams.

Dorita was a lovely, freckled seventeen-year-old brunette with a sassy demeanor. Mary, by now fifteen, was a slim, shapely, black-haired, and blue-eyed teenager. Both girls were embarking on their journey of fascination with boys. The girls would never miss their favorite TV show, *Bonanza,* because of the handsome actors.

"Adam Cartwright is mine!" Dorita would claim.

"Little Joe is mine!" Mary would respond.

Gladys, who was still too young at age twelve to enter these debates, agreed to settle for Hoss Cartwright, who was lovable although slightly chubby.

For teenagers, life proceeded under hardship but with minimum worries, while parents strived to provide them with a semblance of normalcy and joy. The girls soon attracted three young boys from the neighborhood. Yoyo, the oldest boy, cruised around in a vintage 1958 light blue Mustang alongside his pals. After school and on weekends, they embarked on leisurely drives through the neighborhood.

These respectful young boys formed the habit of dropping by the Barrio residence. Sometimes, up to three times on a given day. They stopped, said hello, giggled a little with the girls, and left promptly.

Dorita hatched an idea, "Let's make *polvorones* (a type of cookie that crumbles in your mouth) to treat the boys."

Saturday, then, became a ritual of crafting goodies for the boys, accompanied by subtle enhancements to the girls' appearance—a touch of pale lipstick, rosy cheeks, and charming outfits. The boys, who were sixteen and seventeen, were a blend of bashfulness and excitement. Their arrival was announced by a gentle honk followed by expectant anticipation. The girls would appear at the door, and the interaction varied from a simple wave to brief chuckles and laughs. If the girls walked out showing their baked treats on a tray, their stay would be prolonged with animated conversations around the tasting of the delicacies. Rarely would they walk into the house.

Since Dorita had been a student in Cuba at the *School of the Sacred Heart of Jesus*, Alfredo and Enedina decided to pay a visit to a nearby Catholic school run by nuns of the same religious order. Mother Principal welcomed them as family and said, "Please, bring the three girls to our school."

"We can't, Sister," Alfredo replied. "The tuition is beyond our means. We can barely make ends meet with my salary. Recently, I landed a better paying position, but it still is not enough for us, and the recently arrived extended family."

"We will provide scholarships for the three girls," responded the principal with a loving smile. "We embrace our students from anywhere in the world."

Tears of emotion shone in Alfredo and Enedina's eyes. Everyone except Mary was ecstatic. Mary, having savored the freedom of a co-ed American school, was reluctant to return to the disciplinary environment of an all-girl European nun's school.

"No! I'm not going to that school!" Mary shouted that evening.

To which her parents calmly responded, "You are attending the school that we decide its best for you. So, calm down, and let's move on."

"I don't know why they forced me out of my favorite school. That was the best school I've ever attended. It's not fair to return to the discipline of the nuns." A complaint that Mary would surely carry through her later years.

When asked, "Mary, why is that school so great? What did you learn?" Mary's response was candid—she didn't recall the specifics, but the presence of boys had lent a vibrant charm to her educational experience.

A year after the cousins' arrival, a new chapter began for their family as the parents, Pucho and Dora, accompanied by their youngest daughter, Lourdes, and ten-year-old nephew, Rober, departed Cuba with a temporary destination to

Santander, Spain.

Their journey was a complex ordeal, one they could never have fathomed or foreseen.

24

LETTERS FROM ROBER[29]

Madrid, Spain.
1963

Rober sent the following letters to his family in Cuba.

November 1, 1963

Dear Mom, Dad, and Freddy,

This was our first night here in Spain, and I already miss you so much! Leaving Havana was very sad for me. I wish I could have hugged you longer. I was frightened and down. I know you explained that leaving for Spain with my uncle and his family was best for me. Mom, I'm trying to be brave as you told me, but I'm scared.

At the Havana airport, that scary room surrounded by glass where we were separated gave me goosebumps. It was so hot in there. Now I understand why everyone called it the dreaded *Pecera* - the fishbowl. You feel exactly like a trapped fish looking through the glass. Tío Pucho, Tía Dora and my cousin, Lourditas, we all felt the same, trapped as fish. I wanted to cry looking at the three of you behind that glass.

The disgusting *milicianos* - militiamen, asked us questions and checked us thoroughly to confirm that we were not taking anything more than what we were allowed. Tía Dora had to show that the only jewelry she was carrying

132

was her watch, the wedding ring, and one pair of earrings. They touched us everywhere! They thoroughly checked our shoes, looking for money or jewelry hidden inside the heels. Lourditas and I did not say a word as Tío had warned us not to open our mouths.

"Don't complain! Don't say anything," he said. We could get in real trouble if we did. The men and women wearing the green military clothes seemed to like to upset us. Some travelers were mad - some had tears in their eyes. They were grabbing all of their things. I heard a lady saying, "You have taken everything from us. Let me at least take this with me." But the *miliciano* laughed and still kept the lady's jewelry. They made a young girl jump up and down to make sure that she was not hiding anything between her legs. They even checked her private parts. It was horrible!

Figure 14. Rober's Cuban passport, stamped on exit from Cuba on his way to Madrid.

We finally boarded a cool, big modern PAN-AM plane, they called a Super-Constellation. It was amazing. You know how much I like playing with my toy planes. We were so tired from what we had gone through, but I was very excited to see this modern aircraft. We stopped several times during the long flight to Spain. The first stop was in Newfoundland, Canada. The second stop was the beautiful Balearic Islands. I wanted to remember everything I saw so that I could tell you. After about twelve long hours of flight, we finally arrived at the *Barajas Airport* in Madrid.

We got off the plane with no idea where to go. My Tío followed the crowd, and we followed him. We went to the luggage pick-up area, and while waiting for our luggage, Tío Pucho was anxious and worried. I think it was because they did not allow him to bring any money, and he had no idea where to go in this strange place. Suddenly, Mom, it was really like an angel from heaven showed up. A man approached Tío from the back, tapped him on his shoulder, and said, "*¿Pucho, que haces aqui?* - Pucho, what are you doing here?

Mom, Dad, it was a friend from Santiago de Cuba! None of us could believe this, a real miracle! He could have only come from heaven. Tío, opened his eyes wide, bursting with happiness and embraced his friend with great affection.

You are not going to believe this, but this angel, after he heard our story from Tío, took 20,000 pesetas from his pocket and gave it to my uncle! Not only that, he offered to take all of us to a place called a *pension,* which looks like a dorm for students or immigrants. Tío could not be any more grateful and promised to return the money as soon as he could.

As we headed outside the airport towards the car, we felt the cold. It was *so cold.* We had no coats and no warm clothing for this harsh, cold weather. As our friend was driving us through the streets of Madrid, the city looked so gloomy on this very cold, overcast day.

This is a strange city, very different from Santiago de

Cuba—heavy traffic, many different cars, unlike the ones back home. Lots of people wear big warm coats, hats, and gloves. Everyone walks fast up and down the streets. I have never seen anything like this. We don't wear these heavy coats in Santiago de Cuba. I already miss our warm weather and the bright sun.

I'm so tired. I'll write more tomorrow. I love you, and I miss you all so much!

Rober

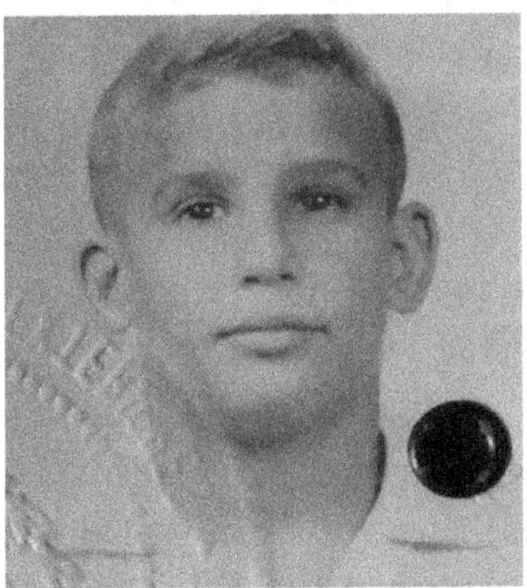

Figure 15. Rober Bory Barrio, 1963.

~ ~ ~

November 4, 1963

Dear Mom, Dad, and Brother,

Last Saturday, our first day here in Madrid, we woke up early and, with the little money that was loaned to Tío, we went to buy coats for the four of us. We could barely sleep that first night. It was so cold! We went to bed wearing as much clothing from our luggage as we could, but nothing was warm enough. There are no heaters in this house. The rooms will only warm up a little when the coal stove is turned on. But a horrendous cold chilled our bones when the stove was turned off. We wished the *pension* manager kept it on all night but they say they can't. It's too expensive and too dangerous to keep it on.

Today is finally Monday, and we can go to the bank. Mom, Dad, did you know that *Abuelo* - grandfather, Manuel had a small bank account here in Madrid? Abuelos Manuel and America used to vacation here in Spain, his homeland, before Fidel took everything away from them. You know how Abuelo was always saving for a rainy day. Well, he kept a small bank account here in Madrid in case of an emergency. Wow, and this was a ¡*tremenda emergencia!* - a huge emergency! This money will help us survive for a few more days.

I know how worried you are about me, so you will be happy to hear this. At the *pension,* someone told us about this place where they serve meals to immigrants. We have been going there every day. It's the Catholic Church that helps Cubans as they arrive here in Madrid. Mom and Dad, even though its cold, they are so nice here at the *pension* and the public dining halls. They have a big room with tables and chairs where they serve food every day. Many Cuban families like us, go to this place. We are lucky to have found this place and these people. Every day before entering the dining room, Tío says, "Make sure to fill your tummies! Remember, we don't have money for any more food." The food is good, not like the one you cook, Mom, but we are hungry, so it tastes good to us. We have at least one good meal every day. I love you all and miss you more every day,

Rober

~ ~ ~

November 8, 1963

Dear Mom, Dad, and Freddy,

The money is running out fast, and Tío Pucho is getting nervous about this. Although the plan is to go soon to Puerto Rico, he got a temporary job at *Bola Roja*, a company that makes tomato sauce. His job is so funny! He stands on the sidewalk outside the store with a clicker in his hand, and when someone walks into the store, he clicks. He clicks, clicks, clicks all day long.

I enrolled in an all-boys school, but to get to this school, my uncle has to take me on the train every morning. The train is always so crowded. Yesterday, at the station, when we were ready to board the train, the crowd pushed me in, and I lost sight of Tío. The door closed, and I saw him getting desperate. I was desperate myself - afraid of getting lost on this train in this confusing city. He spotted me inside, and through the window, he screamed, "Get off at the next stop. I will meet you there!" I was so scared, but glad to hear him in the midst of all that noise. I know I'm not short for my age, but everyone on the train was so much taller than me. I looked up and could only see long arms and coats. I could not reach the upper handles where everyone was holding on, I felt nauseous and scared. The pungent smell of sweat through the old heavy coats, along with no good air, made me feel sick. Finally, when the train came to the next stop, I ran out.

I don't know which was scarier, me trapped inside the train by myself or waiting alone for Tío at that station, surrounded by all those scary people. Time seemed endless. Finally, I saw the next train approaching, and there was him anxiously waving at me through the window. He exited, pushing his way through like a crazy person.

He was very uptight but happy to see me safe.

Love you all,

Rober

~ ~ ~

Ponce, Puerto Rico.
1964-1965

January 18, 1964

Dear Mom, Dad, and Brother,

After three months in Madrid with that terrible cold weather, we finally arrived today in Puerto Rico. Tíos Alfredo and Enedina, and *primos* were waiting for us at the airport. We were so happy to see the family! I love the heat here. Puerto Rico feels like Cuba. I felt like I was back home.

Tío Pucho and Tía Dora did not stop crying and embracing my cousins. They had not seen their children, Dorita and Manolito, in over two years. It was a sad and happy reunion for me. I felt happy for them, but at the same time, jealous that it was not me reuniting with you.

Uncle Alfredo rented a van to transport the ten of us directly to Ponce, the city where they live. We spent hours driving through risky mountains. They call this road *La Piquiña,* which means the itching. Tío told me they named it this way because it is dangerous with sharp turns and giant-size cliffs.

Once we arrived in Ponce, we learned that my Uncle Alfredo had rented a house for us in a neighborhood called Constancia. It's not as nice as where we live in Santiago, but it's close to the rest of the family and near the school we'll be attending. I overheard a conversation. They were discussing how expensive catholic schools are. Luckily, the girls have been given a scholarship, but they still have to pay for Manolito and me. I heard them saying, "We have to give them a good education, especially now that they lost everything and that we have to start all over again."

Love you and miss you!

Rober

~~~

<div style="text-align: right">March 15, 1964</div>

Dear Mom and Dad,

I miss you a lot. My aunt and uncle give me love, but it is not the same without you. Please, try to come soon. We are trying to do all we can to request your entrance to this country. I miss you a lot.

In Ponce, the weather is muggy and hot. with mosquitos everywhere, all day and night long. We have no air conditioning. I'm grateful my uncle bought me an electric fan. I can sleep better now. Some houses have screens on their windows, but we don't. I get bitten all night long.

Remember the horsy that you said that you are buying for me when you get here? I can't stop thinking about it. Just like Silba, right? My dear horsy from Ciudamar? Do you know that his name was really "Silver" which means Plata like metal? Not Silba, which means whistle. Now that I'm learning English, I realize that I always had his name wrong. It was never Whistle.

In school everything is ok. I have new friends, and I will be joining the Boy Scouts soon. It's like the *Pioneritos* in Cuba but without the communist teachings as they do it there.

Rober

~~~

April 10, 1964

Dear Mom, Dad, and Freddy,

Why are you taking so long? My uncles tell me that you are doing everything in your power to come. I know that in your last letter, you told me that it was not your fault. I heard Tío saying that requirements are made harsher every day. I even signed a paper as a minor son requesting you here. Why don't they let you come?

Did you know that my Uncle Alfredo, Aunt Enedina, and cousins, Mary and Gladys, left Ponce to live in San Juan? Now, I not only miss you, but I also miss them. Tío Alfredo explained that they were leaving because he is going to start his own business. He had a good job here in Ponce, but you know how he is. He wants his own business. He works very hard. He is going to do well, but I miss them so much.

I was promised that I would spend summers with them in San Juan and I'm so looking forward to that. I love to spend time with them. In San Juan, I can go to many places with my cousins. We go to the movies, and I am the one who chaperones my cousin Mary with her boyfriend, Ubal, who is the son of one of your friends from Santiago. Remember them?

I love it when I'm asked to chaperone. We go to the beach or for ice cream, and you know what? Ubal gives me money to buy extra ice cream so that I leave them alone for a while so that he can kiss her. I saw them kissing!

Luisito, Ubal's younger brother, is planning to film a movie with his camera, and he is writing the script for it. We are all going to be the actors. The movie will be called *The Two Personalities of Marcia Wimbledon.* It's about an inheritance. Mary and Ubal will be the couple inheriting the money. All of us will have a role in the movie. I will play the servant, and Virgina, Ubal's younger sister, is the murderer. I can't wait!

Love you!

Rober

~~~

<div style="text-align: right">June 15, 1964</div>

Dear Mom, Dad, and Freddy,

I'm punished! We are all punished here except Lourdes. I got bad grades in school, D+ and C- but not only that, I know I did something bad. I tried with my cousins Dorita and Manolito to forge my uncle's signature on the report card, and we were caught. I deserve to be punished. Sorry, Mom and Dad. I promise I'll study more next year and I'll get better grades. I'll make you proud.

Love,

Rober

~~~

January 7, 1965

Dear Mom, Dad, and Freddy,

The Three Kings left me a bike! A brand-new bike! It's beautiful! I'm so excited! This is a short letter because I'm going out to ride my bike now. The bike is called "Camella" and it's gold!

Now I can ride my bike to school, and I don't have to walk that long anymore. I'm so happy!

Love,

Rober

~~~
~~~

March 15, 1965

Dear Mom, Dad, and Freddy,

I'm so sad! I left my bike for a minute across from the bakery, and it was stolen! I'm so mad! I don't know how to tell my uncle. I'm so worried. He is going to be sad and angry. They put so much effort into getting us things. Losing something so expensive is horrible! It's so unfair! I knew things get stolen around here, and that's why there are iron bars in all houses.

I don't know what to do,
Rober

~ ~ ~

November 1, 1965

Dear Mom, Dad, and Brother,

I'm so happy! I heard that you've received permission to leave Cuba! I can't wait to see you! I was told that *Abuela* America is also coming with you! I can't wait to see Grandma! She is so old and I love her so much. I'm so glad she is coming. Tío told me that you will be going to Miami first. When I heard the news, I ran to write this letter, just to let you know how happy I am and that I can't wait. I have been dreaming of this moment and I can't believe it's here now!

Do you know that we are not going to live here in Ponce? We will be living in San Juan with Tío Alfredo and his family. I prefer San Juan; we can live better and have more fun there than in Ponce.

I have grown so much since you last saw me that you will not recognize me. It's been three years. I can't believe I'm thirteen years old and haven't seen you in so long. I keep growing and getting taller. I inherited my cousins' clothing and shoes since mine became tight on me fast.

I know how sad it must be for you to leave behind all the things that you love, our beautiful home, your cherished *adornitos* - decorations, furniture, and jewelry. Everything gone! How unfair! I was told that on top of them stealing everything from us, they are asking you to pay $400 because your freezer broke!

Tío Alfredo already rented a house for us in a neighborhood called Villa Nevarez. He is getting the house ready with beds, a table, chairs, and food! Do you know, Mom and Dad, that Tío Alfredo has done this for many families which arrive penniless from Cuba?

This area of San Juan is called Rio Piedras. I have been told that I will finish the semester here in Ponce and then I will move to San Juan where I will attend a public school named Sotero Figueroa. I will miss my friends here but knowing that you are coming makes up for all sadness.

Today I saw a beautiful rainbow in the sky and I thought, "That's exactly how I feel, happy as a rainbow. My family is arriving soon!"

I can't wait to hug you!

Rober

~~~

From that moment forward, Alfredo assumed the financial responsibility for the newly arriving extended family, as Cuba's rules prohibited anyone from leaving with money in their pockets.

A few years later, Pilar fondly recalled, "Alfredo provided not only shelter, which sometimes meant renting a home, but also stocked refrigerators, offered initial financial support, and secured job opportunities for every family
~~~

member. He even covered the down payment for our first home in Puerto Rico."

~~~

Upon Dorita and Manolito's parents and little sister Lourdes' arrival, the family of five reunited and settled in Ponce, Puerto Rico. Following his father Manuel's footsteps, Pucho established a prosperous furniture and rental business. Although the longing for their beloved homeland never waned in their hearts, they led a tranquil and comfortable life in Ponce until the end of their days.
~~~

25

PONCE EASTER SURPRISE
Ponce, Puerto Rico.
1965

"Eni, look at those people, don't they look like…?"

Alfredo's comment was cut short by a voice calling out their names.

"Alfredo! Eni!"

Nestled in the picturesque hills of Cerro del Vigia, overlooking the majestic city of Ponce, lay the opulent Serralles' mansion, home of the owners *Serralles' Distillery*, renowned for producing the famous *Don Q Rum*. Every spring, The Ponce Intercontinental Hotel, perched on the same hill of Cerro del Vigia, hosted the eagerly anticipated and well-attended traditional Easter Celebration.

On Easter Sundays, the hotel held an *Easter Hat Parade* followed by children's games and an exquisite luncheon. The event featured colorful spring flowers, elegant ladies in beautiful linen and lace dresses, joyous reunions with friends, and a ballroom adorned in pastel hues of spring. The high-society women of Ponce awaited this occasion to showcase their exotic hat creations and exquisite wardrobe, competing for prizes awarded to the most original designs. The event took place in a vast, luxurious ballroom with glass windows and doors that opened to the refreshing breeze and breathtaking views of the hills overlooking the colonial town.

On this particular day, March 29, 1965, Enedina and her daughters donned modest Easter hats, though most of the hats at the celebration were extravagantly ornate.

"Miguel! What are you doing here?" They couldn't believe their eyes.

Miguel Arias, Alfredo's childhood friend from Santiago de Cuba, whom they hadn't seen in several years, stood before them. Miguel, accompanied by his wife Hortensia and their three boys, ages fifteen to nineteen, as well as their twelve-year-old daughter, had made an unexpected entrance to this remote location in a southern corner of the island. Both Miguel and Alfredo were far from where they had grown up, played, and shared countless childhood memories.

"Wow! How did you end up here? What a surprise!" Alfredo struggled to find the right words, the astonishment clear on his face. The friends embraced, overcome with emotion at their unexpected reunion.

"We flew from Cuba to Miami first, then relocated to Puerto Rico. When we heard you were living here, in Ponce, we traveled all the way to see you," explained Miguel, continuing his story.

"But, but." Alfredo, still taken aback by the surprise, couldn't express himself fully.

"Who gave you my address? We are not even home now."

"One of your neighbors, Maricusa, I believe her name is. She told us where to find you. After such a long ordeal, we couldn't leave without seeing you and your family."

"Please, join us at the table, we'll bring more chairs. The

kids can get acquainted out on the terrace," Eni offered.

"We don't want to intrude on your party." Hortensia hesitated, feeling somewhat embarrassed.

"No, not at all! This is the most delightful surprise. You have no idea how happy we are to see all of you. And the kids have grown up so much; they were little when we last saw you in Havana. We have so much catching up to do."

The boys were excited to see the lovely sisters, Mary and Gladys. Mary was particularly taken with how handsome the boys had become. Ubaldo, the middle brother with striking green eyes, immediately caught sixteen-year-old Mary's attention. Luis, the youngest of the boys, proved to be the most outgoing and engaged in lively conversation with the girls.

"We sent the boys first to the US through *Operation Pedro Pan*, organized by the Catholic Church," Miguel explained.

Operation Pedro Pan[30] was a clandestine mass exodus of over 14,000 unaccompanied Cuban minors ages 6 to 18 to the United States over a two-year span from 1960 to 1962. They were sent by their parents, who were alarmed by rumors circulating amongst Cuban families that the new government under Fidel Castro was planning to terminate parental rights and place minors in communist indoctrination centers. Father Bryan O. Walsh of the *Catholic Welfare Bureau* created the program to provide air transportation to the United States for Cuban children. The operation was the largest mass exodus of minor refugees in the Western Hemisphere at the time.

"Wow, Miguel, that must have been a courageous decision."

"No, we were just as panicked as you were. We didn't know what to do and were desperate to ensure the children's safety. Unable to leave Cuba, we seized the opportunity provided by the Catholic Church as a way out. Thankfully, it worked out for us." Miguel shared. "We know *Operation Pedro Pan* was a significant ordeal for many Cuban families like ours. Some boys ended up in different states, many in Texas, with various families. Ubaldo stayed in a children's home in Miami, and my son Miguel Jr. was sent north to live with a family. We were fortunate to reunite in just over a year."

"Are you living in San Juan now? Are you working? What are you doing?" Enedina persisted with her questions.

Meanwhile, the kids enjoyed their conversation on the hotel balcony, surrounded by the picturesque scenery. Luisito, the family's jovial clown, entertained the girls with various tales, "Have you tried the new enormous hamburger? It's called a Whopper! I have never seen anything this big! And coming from Cuba, where food is so scarce, you can imagine! It's crazy!" Their laughter resonated on the terrace, embraced by the fresh spring breeze and the breathtaking view of the hill.

Luisito had the charisma of a comedian and loved making people laugh. Not shy at all, he knew he had a talent for it. Mary, on the other hand, observed Ubaldo from the corner of her eye. Their fate has brought them together to this remote corner of the world, perhaps with a purpose, perhaps to rekindle childhood friendships, perhaps to forge future connections. Maybe, just maybe, the universe was conspiring to align two lives, two families, forever.

26

CAN WE START ONCE MORE?

Ponce to San Juan, Puerto Rico.
1965

Alfredo had dedicated several years of his life to working for the branch of *Glidden Enterprises* based in Ponce, Puerto Rico. During his tenure, he successfully turned around the branch from a state of bankruptcy to a thriving and profitable business. However, despite his achievements, a longing for independence and entrepreneurship began to simmer within him.

"I appreciate this opportunity immensely, but deep down, I have always known I wasn't meant to work for someone else," he confided. "I've enjoyed the growth and financial stability it provided, but now, it's time for me to chart my own course."

Enedina, however, was content with their life in Ponce, a town she found both beautiful and serene. She cherished the friendly and cultured people, the peacefulness, and the financial stability they had finally achieved since leaving Cuba.

"Please, Alfredo," she implored, "we've found a peaceful life here. Ponce is such a beautiful town, and our neighbors have become friends. I'm part of a club for the first time in my life. People are so friendly, they are cultured and at the same time so humble. It's so amazing to live here.

149

Never in my life have I experienced such peace. And for the first time since we left Cuba, we have financial stability. Our daughters are thriving in the best school, and we are living a comfortable life. Let's not upend it all again. I can't bear the thought of starting over. We all love it here."

Alfredo, undeterred by her pleas, sought to persuade her. "I believe we can have even greater things. When you work for someone else, there is a limit to what you can achieve. When you work for yourself, there are no bounds—you set your own limits. You think that this is great because you have erased the best year of your life from your memory. I understand your reluctance to revisit the past, but I can't spend the rest of my life working for someone else." He knew what he wanted from life, and his self-assuredness never wavered. "I delivered on my commitment to them," he affirmed, reflecting on his achievement of reviving their business from the brink of bankruptcy to a thriving enterprise. "You understand that this is where I truly excel. I thrive in the challenge of constructing something substantial from the ground up and achieving success. Once that objective is realized, I get bored, and I need to move on in search of new horizons."

Enedina had seen this coming; she knew her husband well. Yet, she was unwilling to accept this reality. Her life had been marked with upheaval and hardship, and now she craved stability and peace.

"Where are we going? What's the plan?" Eni asked, exhausted and frustrated.

"Miguel and I are starting a business," Alfredo revealed. "Miguel has always been involved in the glass business. He's a bit eccentric but a creative man who makes beautiful glass creations. Furthermore, there's a significant demand here in Puerto Rico for glass and aluminum products. San Juan is growing rapidly, and they currently import glass doors and windows for new constructions. There is a vast opportunity in this industry."

A few weeks later, the family made the move back to San Juan, Puerto Rico. They settled in Rio Piedras, an area close to the University of Puerto Rico, offering their daughters the prospect of attending college there.

As Mary left Ponce, she couldn't help but be thrilled about reuniting with Ubaldo, her now boyfriend, in San Juan. However, for Enedina and Gladys, tears welled up. Some of their happiest memories were entwined with the charm of the colonial town of Ponce.

During the drive to San Juan, Gladys reflected over her emotional journey from an innocent girl to a teenager. She remembered a particular Saturday afternoon at the Ponce Yacht Club with her friends when everything changed. *I suddenly wanted to stand up straight. I wanted to look slim.* She reminisced. *I adjusted my hair while watching the boys my age from afar. They looked different to me that day. I even giggled with my girlfriends, trying to catch their attention.*

Days later, when Gladys confided her story with her romantic Tía Olguita, she summed it up, "The cocoon was metamorphosing into a butterfly,"

Gladys agreed with a bashful smile and a gentle affirmative movement of her head. "Yes, something happened to me that day. Something changed inside of me. I even know the exact moment when it happened! I even remember what I was wearing that day. Before, I'd see girls giggling at boys and thought it was so silly! But that day, I found myself doing the same."

Aunt and niece shared laughter and hugs, "I giggled, trying to get the boys' attention. You know, Tía, I remember how my sister Mary and cousin Dorita used to giggle and get excited when those three boys drove by our home every Saturday and Sunday. I thought they were so foolish!"

Tia Olguita, who had never had children of her own, felt a special connection with her niece, "Maybe there is a little bit of me in you," she mused, embracing her beloved niece. "*Tu eres la niña de mis ojos.* - You are the apple of my eye."

27

THE DREADED INSPECTION
Santiago de Cuba, Cuba.
1965

"Freddy, please remember not to talk to anyone in school about what we have in the house and our upcoming plans; it's dangerous. We no longer know who anyone really is," Pilar said to her younger son as she was putting him to bed that night.

"But Mom, what about my best friend Alex?"

"Freddy, please, no one. We don't know." Pilar pleaded with fear and compassion.

"But they know that my brother Rober already left Cuba."

"We have been telling anyone who asks that he went to the US to study for a year."

"Ok, Mom. I won't tell anyone, but I hate to live like this."

"We all hate to live like this, but it's the only way to survive. Hopefully, this will not last too long. Hopefully." Pilar sighed as she exited the room.

Six years had passed since the dreadful day that Batista fled the island, and the country was taken over by the bearded militia who had promised improvements but brought only grief and desolation. For four appalling years Roberto, as the attorney he was, had to witness the

153

confiscation of properties and testify and pronounce dead those killed by the brutal militia. He couldn't take it anymore. But Fidel Castro would fill his mouth with sarcasm to say, "With the revolution, everything, but outside the revolution, nothing!" Those outside the revolution could not keep a job or feed their families, or even get access to food and medications. Those wanting to survive had to either be with the revolution or at least fake their alliance. However, the CDR knew and kept a close eye on those they suspected of being *gusanos* – worms, the counterrevolutionaries.

"Roberto, tomorrow is our home's government inspection." Pilar's pulse began to race merely at the thought of this ghastly experience. They want to make sure that we don't give away, or take, or hide anything." Roberto replied.

"Ever since we requested permission to leave the country, we are labeled as *gusanos*. They are vigilant day and night to ensure we don't move anything out of the house. I see them looking this way, watching continuously, outside and through the windows." Pilar continued while looking out the window.

"Pilar, the ongoing surveillance has been happening longer than you think. Even before we requested documents to leave the country. They know who we are. They know who is with the revolution and who's not. They are no fools."

"I wonder if maybe, deep inside, they are just like us but keep faking their alliance with the regime only to survive themselves." Pilar pondered.

"Envy and resentment! Our new neighbors had very few possessions, and now, you see, they were given that good house with the furniture and decorations of our old neighbors. Everything our old neighbors worked for all their lives now belongs to these people who do not even know how to appreciate and preserve. They are destroying everything. Since they did not have to work for it, they don't value it. Of course, they want to work for the communist government, spying on the neighbors for the adulterated revolution," Roberto could not hide his own resentment.

"I feel like I'm in jail." Thirty-eight-year-old Pilar commented in disbelief. "We are prisoners in our own homes. Oh, no, here they are! The truck is there with about five of them." Pilar alerted Roberto that morning with tension rushing through her veins.

"Roberto, please control yourself. It's hard, but we have to be polite. Otherwise, they will not let us leave the country."

A loud knock was heard at the front door. Pilar walked slowly toward the door while Roberto stayed behind, trying to calm down. The glare of the morning sun filtering through the porch prevented her from clearly seeing their faces.

"Good morning," Pilar greeted them politely with sadness in her voice.

"We are here for the inspection!" One of the men said. Five of them, all wearing wrinkled olive-green fatigues and dirty old knee-high black boots, tramped into the house without an invitation.

"Are you Roberto Bory, the ex-owner of this house?" One of them asked with a cynical smile while looking at his colleagues, sharing with a gesture the mocking situation.

"Yes, I'm *El Licenciado* – attorney, Roberto Bory," Roberto responded defiantly. Pilar opened her eyes wide at her husband, trying with her gaze to remind him to calm down.

"Hey you, Carlos, Juan, Jose, take inventory of the bedrooms. Fernando, take the dining room and family room. I'll take the kitchen and living room," he said, dispatching his men to other rooms. "Make sure to write down every single item, table, chest, painting, picture frame, and chair. Everything. And please emphasize the most valuable items." He stopped to laugh. "Well, that is if you can recognize them." He even mocked his own recruits.

Pilar was relieved to know that this was happening while their son Freddy was in school. She wanted to spare him from this cruel and humiliating experience. Pilar and Roberto felt sick knowing that these dirty, disgusting men were touching and mishandling their precious property with filthy hands. Every corner of the house was carefully inspected and recorded. Every piece of furniture that the family bought with so much effort and hard work and that meant so much to them was now treated as rubbish.

"This chest looks expensive!" Federico looked at Roberto while rubbing his hand through the top and side of the chest. "Was this custom-made, or is it one of those expensive brands?"

"My father owned a furniture store. That piece was a wedding gift." Pilar jumped in, trying to answer as briefly as possible, hoping to hide her indignation and being perceived as resisting the inspection.

All business in Pilar's family had been previously confiscated by the government during the first years of the revolution. *Muebleria Barrio*, the large furniture store her father had built, was confiscated shortly after the revolution. She blamed her father's death on the distress caused by the communist government. His brother Alfredo's hardware business, a successful Havana establishment, was also confiscated by the revolution. These businesses were given to unskilled individuals from the communist party who had no knowledge of how to run them. Soon, these flourishing businesses went bankrupt and were destroyed or had to close down. Roberto was able to work as an attorney with the government for a while longer, but as soon as he was labeled as anti-communist, anti-revolutionary, and an enemy of the regime, all benefits were taken away. It was even difficult to find food for his family.

At this point, it was excruciatingly painful to turn all their lifetime properties into the government. However, they had no choice. They had no option but to flee the country.

On the day of their scheduled departure, the same five *milicianos*, dressed in the same grimy olive-green fatigues and mud-caked boots, arrived early in the morning. As they entered the house, their pungent sweat permeated the air. Pilar, Roberto, and Freddy felt a growing sense of nausea. They greeted the men with caution, well aware of the final inspection that stood between them and their escape from the country. They have heard of their friend Pura, whose mother suffered a fatal heart attack during the last inspection, unable to bear the unbearable tension of this painful ordeal.

The family's luggage, limited to one piece per person, stood ready by the main door. The men strode in with brutish attitudes, relishing their control over the situation. They dispersed throughout the house, their intentions clear.

"Where is the crucifix?" Federico, the leader of the minuteman, demanded.

Pilar and Roberto exchanged astonishing glances.

"Which crucifix?" Pilar asked, her voice trembling.

"Don't act as if you don't know," The unpleasant man retorted, approaching her with a menacing attitude. "The big standing crucifix that was on this table," he yelled.

"I'm sorry, but since religion has been eradicated from the country, we didn't think that you would be interested in a crucifix," Pilar managed to say.

"Where is it!" He demanded impatiently.

"A relative of ours has taken it."

"It must be returned right now! No one is leaving this country until that crucifix is returned!" he bellowed with arrogance.

"Don't worry, I'll call right now, and it will be returned," Roberto responded, trying to soothe the situation. "We did not think that you would be interested in this item," he added, his thoughts veering toward the real motive behind this intimidation.

"Pilar, stay calm. They are not going to win this war. We are leaving this country today. They are trying to humiliate us. Let them play their game. We will also play ours," Roberto whispered into Pilar's ear.

"Where is all the clothing that was hanging in this closet? We know that you are not taking it with you. You are only allowed to take three pieces of clothing, and this closet was filled during our first inspection! Where is it?" Carlos, in charge of the bedroom inventory, demanded furiously. Pilar and Roberto were left speechless.

Meanwhile, young Freddy hid in a corner of the room, terror-stricken. *They are not going to let us go. I will never see my brother again. We will starve to death or maybe put into prison,* he thought as he tried to quell the tremors coursing through his body and the tears streaming down his cheeks.

Roberto, experienced in dealing with such tormentors, spoke calmly, "Tell me what you would like to see in the closet, and we will replace it."

"What you will have to replace is the refrigerator. It was working during the initial inspection. Aha! And now, what a coincidence it's broken!" Federico exclaimed sarcastically as he entered the room.

At this point, Pilar and her son were in total panic, struggling to conceal their anxiety.

"Listen, just tell me what you want," Roberto conceded his determination to resolve the situation unwavering despite his defeat.

"Well," Federico strutted toward Roberto with an air of arrogance. "To start, you will have to pay $400 for the broken refrigerator."

"Four hundred dollars! You must be joking!" Roberto exclaimed, disbelief in his voice. This was the 1960s when $400 was considered a small fortune.

"Well, if you don't have the money, you and your family will not leave!" Federico declared triumphantly, turning around to exchange smirks with his colleagues.

Time was running out. Roberto had to find the money, and Pilar had to make phone calls to arrange for the return of the crucifix and the clothing they had removed from the closet. They had a plane to catch, and the airport promised more intrusive and humiliating inspections that would require several hours.

~~~
~~~

That evening, as night descended upon the land, dusk painted the sky with tinted bands of hazy lavender along the horizon and dark purple, almost black clouds floating above. The Bory family soared over their beautiful island for the last time, gazing out of the aircraft window with tears in their eyes. The turquoise waters of the Caribbean beaches and the lush green mountains that witnessed their youth faded into the distance. The streets of Santiago de Cuba vanished from view as they left their hearts behind. Fearful thoughts raided their imaginations: *What will await us? Penniless. Nothing. Starting all over again!*

"We will return, Freddy, I promise you. We will return!" Pilar said, attempting to console her son while trying to etch the beauty of the island into her memory forever. Little did they know that this was the last time they would lay eyes on their beloved Pearl of the Sea.

28

CAN YOU HELP US OUT, PLEASE?

1965-1966

During this period, Alfredo was frequently approached with a common plea from friends and family still trapped in Cuba:

"Can you help us out, please? We are afraid for our kids. Our boys and girls are reaching critical ages: military age for the boys and mandatory sugar cane field service for our girls."

During these short conversations, friends spoke with strained voices, fearful of being overheard and charged as contra-revolutionaries if their phones were tapped. They shared the news that people disappear from the streets daily, neighborhood informants are constantly on the lookout, and any mention of discontent with the government is met with imprisonment, torture, forced labor, or death.

News and comments from Cuba kept flowing continuously:

"We live in fear. We have to hide to pray. Priest and nuns have been exiled from the island."

Including statements like:

"We never know what we are eating the next day. We spend all day in long lines to get a few eggs; then we must join another long line for chicken. All hours of the day are spent in search of food."

"We cannot even find the items we are supposed to get with la *Libreta de Abastecimientos* – the food rationing booklet."

We hear that when the government says: "Today we have eggs in Marianao!" Everyone runs in that direction.

Interestingly, there is not even paper in Cuba to print the rationing cards.

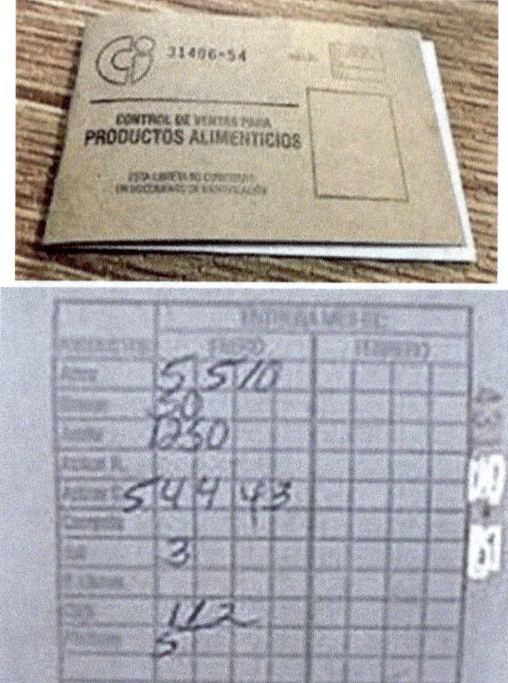

Figure 16. *Libreta de Abastecimientos (ration cards.)*

One of the jokes heard on the streets is:

"What is the animal with the longest tail in Cuba?"

The answer:

The chicken, because of the long lines formed when they announce poultry availability. (In Spanish, the word for tail – *cola,* is the same as for a line of people.)

So, those in that miserable predicament could laugh and say they're in *"La cola del pollo* - the tail of the chicken" when waiting in a long line to get poultry.

One of the Spanish TV stations reported that chickens were injected with water to make them heavier.

And that milk is only for families with babies. And you don't even get enough milk for one baby.

Also, people are grinding mops to make *picadillo*-ground meat. This is how hungry they are. The never-ending, unbelievable, sad remarks continued.

~ ~ ~

Alfredo was on the phone talking to someone in Cuba. When he hung up, Gladys said, "Dad, Castro's communist regime intentionally keeps people focused on survival, building a generation of non-thinkers and preventing them from rebelling or seeking change."

"I wholeheartedly agree," Alfredo responded. "I just concluded a phone call with a friend who requested that I dispatch automotive components to him because he had been without a car for months. Parts can't be found on the island."

He added that news kept flowing through the radio in Puerto Rico, saying that people were dying of lack of medicines and limited medical facilities, adding, "But, who can survive with a salary of $28 dollars a month for a doctor? $5 or $10 a month for most people?"

"Eni, how can I deny them help? My heart goes out to them. I lived through that. Now is my turn to help," Alfredo had never denied assistance to anyone. His unwavering support extended to both family and friends in their times of need. Through this tunnel of hope, he gradually brought all his close relatives to Puerto Rico, answering their pleas for assistance one by one.

Cristalum, the glass and aluminum company Alfredo and Miguel started in San Juan, Puerto Rico, provided work and salaries to many new arrivals.

Bautista and Maria, both in their sixties, were the heads of the resilient Castañer family who endured the harrowing bombardments of the Spanish Civil War and were previously compelled to exile from Spain to Cuba three decades ago. Now, they found themselves in their second exile. Aurora, the beautiful and talented Castañer sister, had arrived in Puerto Rico in 1961. Her toll as a baker, with unending hours of hard work had etched upon her face the trials she had endured. Youth and beauty had slipped away like an old friend, once a constant presence but now relegated to a distant memory.

Enedina's eldest brother, Alfred Castañer (El Gallego), along with his wife Ileana and their two children, Luis and Ileanita, had joined the family in November of 1966. Both Gallego and Roman Castañer, skilled accountants by profession, temporarily shared the accounting duties at *Cristalum*. The older brother remained as the company's accountant, while Roman seized a promotion opportunity with another firm.

"Gallego, I'm in the process of submitting applications and pursuing the necessary courses to revalidate my teaching career. I intend to secure a position at our children's elementary/middle school," Ileana declared, wasting no time in her determined quest to regain her footing.

Pilar, Alfredo's sister, served as the customer care representative at *Cristalum*, and she greeted every customer who entered with a "How can I help you?"

"During that time, although we didn't have a penny, we were so happy. The family was together, and we found ways to meet and have fun without money," Enedina reflected years later.

Almost every Sunday, Ileana and Gallego made rice and black beans, while Roman and Olguita brought fried plantains and dessert. Pilar added pork, salad, and drinks.

"Oh! Ileana, don't forget the guitar." Enedina enthusiastically planned the low-cost family outings. The younger kids and teenagers play all day long in the soft white sand and turquoise waters, where the family spends memorable, joyous days on the delightful Caribbean beaches of Puerto Rico. This was the financially affordable entertainment that this big, happy family of poor immigrants could afford.

"In the absence of our beloved island of Cuba, this sister island of Puerto Rico offered us the home we had lost. This island gave us hope, gave us a roof, gave us love and the joy that we thought we had lost forever. It offered us a brighter future for us and our children," Alfredo declared with pride, joy, and satisfaction of the life he had regained for himself, his family, and friends in this welcoming country.

Years later, Enedina remarked with a smile, "You know, I think we had the most fun when we were poor."

29

THE SEED WE PLANTED

Río Piedras, Puerto Rico.
1968

Gladys inquired of a fellow Chemistry 101 classmate as they strolled through the hallway, "Why is Dr. Nestor Rodriguez's office always so crowded?"

"Come with me, and you will find out!" her friend replied, leading the way toward the office.

"Come on in!" Dr. Rodriguez warmly called out from his desk, beckoning the curious young ladies who had peered into his office. "It's Friday afternoon, and this is when I deliver my most captivating lesson - the chemistry of beer brewing." Laughter filled the room.

"Beer brewing?" Gladys questioned in astonishment. *I knew he was a little different,* she thought but, "Well? count me in! I'm sorry if I'm a little late for the lesson, but I'm genuinely intrigued," she declared with wide-eyed enthusiasm.

The students already inside the office grinned and made room for the newcomers as Gladys and her friend squeezed into the bustling space.

"As you'll soon discover, the distillation equipment we discussed today in the chemistry lab has some very practical applications," Dr. Rodriguez explained, continuing amid the ongoing giggles and camaraderie.

"That's wonderful!" Gladys exclaimed.

Later that afternoon, as she entered her home, she approached her father saying, "You know Dad, I think I've figured out what I want to major in."

The family was getting ready for dinner, and Gladys went to wash up before returning to help set the table. The enticing aroma of *fricase de pollo* - chicken fricassee, white rice, and *tostones* - fried green plantains, filled the air of the dining room.

"So, how was school? Have you decided on a major?" her dad inquired. Gladys was currently enrolled in foundational coursework at the *University of Puerto Rico.*

"Well, you know that I've always been interested in many subjects, so it's been hard to choose," Gladys began. "I was leaning toward social work, particularly working with children with disabilities. I've been volunteering in that area, and I really enjoy it. However, today, something unique happened that filled me with excitement." Her body language exuded enthusiasm.

"Well, tell us!" Enedina urged eagerly. "Why are you hesitating?"

"I don't know, maybe because it might sound strange." Gladys responded.

"Why? Just say it." Alfredo encouraged. At this point Alfredo and Enedina were barely eating their dinner, their eyes fixed on their daughter, impatiently awaiting her news.

"Well, I think I want to become a scientist! Perhaps a chemist." Gladys declared, her hands flying to her face in elation as she peered at her parents through the top of her eyes.

Smiles illuminated their faces, and after a few moments

of silence, Alfredo said, "So, you remembered!"

Perplexed by this response and sporting a look of intrigue, Gladys inquired, "Remembered what?"

A decade earlier, while Alfredo was launching his business in Havana, he encountered a specific demand among his clients. "Alejo, I have clients who need a robust adhesive for bonding new Formica to wood, creating a finishing touch for kitchen cabinets. They are selling Formica-finished cabinets, and people complain that the tops are coming off."

Alfredo had scoured catalogs searching for a solution to his client's dilemma. "There is a new product in the United States, recently developed, that might do the trick. DuPont manufactures this adhesive. I'm contacting them to see if they can send me a sample for testing." This notion eventually propelled them to become the island's top distributor of what they christened *Duroplasty*.

"But one day," Alfredo continued, "when you were just eight years old, I told you, 'One day, you're going to be the chemist in my laboratory. You'll be the scientist crafting the raw material for this kind of adhesive.'"

"Dad, I don't recall any of this," Gladys admitted as she attempted to unearth memories from the past. "But you know, perhaps, just perhaps, that idea lay dormant in the deep recesses of my mind all these years." A contented grin spread across Alfredo's face, and soon, expressions of satisfaction emerged in everyone's faces.

"We're elated with your decision," Alfredo exclaimed joyfully. He reached out to hold his daughter's hand, signifying that her choice couldn't have been more perfect in fulfilling her parents' expectations. "You may no longer be interested in inventing new adhesives, given that we are no longer in that business but, who knows," he paused. "You might invent an artificial *boniato* - sweet potato." Laughter filled the room.

Then, adopting a more serious tone, he added, "You know Eni, this shows that they can strip us of our country, our homes, our businesses, all material possessions, but no one, absolutely no one, can tamper with the seeds of values, education, and dreams that we have planted in our children. Those will thrive within them forever."

30

CULTURAL DIVERGENCE

Miami, Florida.
1978

Gladys exclaimed in response to Alfredo's culture shock "Wow, it's so different here."

"Dad, I told you so," Gladys replied, emphasizing her point as she gestured. She had anticipated Alfredo's reaction to the contrasting attitudes of people of the same nationality in different settings.

Alfredo and Enedina embarked on a new chapter in their lives, relocating from their beloved Puerto Rico to Miami upon their retirement. Their decision to make this move was partly inspired by their youngest daughter, Gladys, who had previously married and settled in Miami to pursue her postgraduate studies in the field of Chemistry.

After observing these cultural differences, Alfredo declared, "The Cuban culture here in Miami is completely different from the one we experienced in Puerto Rico." Alfredo paused, seemingly puzzled, as he continued, "What I feel when I listen to the radio, watch Hispanic TV, and engage in conversations on the streets here in Miami, is as if Castro and the diaspora is a recent event for them, not an exodus that began almost twenty years ago!"

"I know, Dad, you may not remember it, but I mentioned

this to you and Mom right after I moved to Miami five years ago. I underwent the same cultural shock that you are experiencing today."

In 1972, Gladys left the island of Puerto Rico, her home for thirteen years, to attend graduate school in Columbus, Ohio. During her journey, she met an old friend from her hometown who was now living in Miami. A year later, this friend persuaded her to transfer to the University of Miami to complete her doctoral work. Miami, with its tropical weather, sunny days, and beautiful ocean views, was the kind of environment Gladys had always preferred. While she had initially enjoyed her time up north, the harsh cold weather and demanding coursework forced her into confinement within the student dorms. This lifestyle was a far cry from the tropical islands she was accustomed to, prompting her to consider relocation.

The University of Miami offered a combined Master/Ph.D. program during her transfer. She even married her friend who had suggested the move, seeing it as an opportunity for both a Ph.D. and a husband. Later, not only her parents but several other family members relocated to Miami.

"It's astounding to observe how members of the same nationality develop differently in diverse settings," Gladys continued, unable to sit still in her parents' new, brightly decorated living room.

Alfredo acknowledged, "I remember you mentioning it, but it's so different to hear about it than to live it."

Enedina chimed in with nostalgia, "We miss our friends and life in Puerto Rico, but we are happy here, close to you, and we have this beautiful lake house in Kendall.

Recognizing the adverse impact of the deteriorating economy in Puerto Rico, we were compelled to seek a new location for our residence. Additionally, your being here in Miami attracted us to this city. We wanted to be close to you and the upcoming grandkids," Enedina exclaimed with a broad smile, "and our American neighbors are so nice."

"Mom, this is America! Of course, they are American neighbors." Gladys replied with a smile.

Enedina continued, "Well, sometimes it doesn't feel like the US since so many people here speak Spanish. The Hispanic culture here in Miami is different from the original Cuba and from the Cubans living in Puerto Rico. Still, it's hard to describe the differences."

Gladys took in the ambiance of her parents' new home, adorned with memories forged in exile. Her gaze was drawn to replicas of paintings she had acquired during an academic European study trip years ago. On the right wall hung Vann Gogh's *Sun Flowers*, which she remembered picking up in Amsterdam. On the left, Diego Velaquez' *Las Meninas*, purchased at El Museo Del Prado in Madrid.

Memories!

She fantasized for a second about the memorable trip, memories whisking her away into imagination. However, she was rapidly brought back to the reality of the present conversation.

"I feel several factors influenced the drastic differences in the development of Cuban exiles in Miami compared to those like us in Puerto Rico. And I guess, anywhere else where the diaspora may have taken us," Alfredo added, his energy evident as he gestured while speaking.

Pepin, a family friend who walked in for a short visit,

overhearing the conversation, offered his perspective, "Cubans who arrived in Miami without knowing the language were forced to remain in their Cuban enclave, consuming Cuban media, dining at Spanish-speaking restaurants, theaters, supermarkets, and not fully integrating with the broader American community. In Puerto Rico, without the language barrier, we were able to blend in and evolve among the local population."

"We felt like one with our Puerto Rican friends and neighbors. Maybe because I was younger, I really didn't feel any difference among us," Gladys interjected.

"The notable difference is the success rate of professionals." Pepin continued, "While I don't have any specific data, I believe businesspeople like us found success in Spanish-speaking countries, whereas in the U.S., the language barrier posed significant challenges. Only the most resilient individuals could overcome them."

Alfredo, after greeting their guest, reclined in his armchair, pondering the phenomenon they were discussing. "Only those who persevered in learning the language could succeed. Many had to start with factory jobs and low-level positions just to provide for their families."

Gladys added, "Yes, and the Hialeah factories were filled with Cuban exiles."

"That's true! Some remained there, merely securing basic necessities for their families while sending money to relatives in Cuba and waiting for a return that never materialized." Alfredo lamented, his frustration evident.

"The same individuals who landed in Spanish-speaking countries like Puerto Rico with similar education levels were able to secure better jobs due to the absence of the language barrier," Alfredo surmised.

"Some of the professionals who left Cuba at the beginning of the revolution were highly motivated. They learned the language, validated their degrees, and remain successful to this day," Gladys continued. "Look at my father-in-law. He studied the language, revalidated his law degree, and returned to become as successful an attorney as he was in Cuba before Castro."

"The legal system in this country is entirely different, making the transition even more challenging, but he was relentless," Enedina replied.

Gladys recalled other examples, saying, "Yes, and Jesus' dad did the same with his engineering degree."

Alfredo, deep in thought, tried to make sense of their analysis. "I feel that individuals who departed Cuba at the onset of the revolution were more driven to overcome the challenges."

Gladys recounted a story, explaining, "As an example, my manicurist had initially studied a medical career in Cuba, while her husband pursued engineering. Curious, I inquired, 'Have you and your husband considered re-validating your degrees to work in your respective fields here?' Her response remained consistent, 'We don't speak English, lack the financial means to return to college, and we need to work for our survival. We'll explore options for the future, but it's not feasible at the moment.'"

"It's a different mentality. That wasn't the mindset at the onset of the exodus," Alfredo observed, shaking his head, signaling frustration.

Gladys continued, "Years pass, and the doctor spends her life doing nails while the engineer drives a truck or works as a laborer in construction. It's a real shame! I always try to advise them about available programs at the local colleges, but their dire circumstances have led to dashed dreams. I'm uncertain whether it's a matter of circumstance or a lack of motivation." She paused, reflecting on their situation.

Enedina added, "Our friend Nelson mentioned in a recent conversation that new arrivals in Miami are accepting lower living standards."

"Well, that's a different story! The mix of characters and temperaments in our community is truly intriguing. The group that departed for Puerto Rico in the early days of the exodus formed a more cohesive and similar unit."

Alfredo chimed in, a hint of sorrow flickering across his face as he spoke, "It's a consequence of living under a communist regime. In such a system, people come to accept that hard work and personal merit won't lead to a better life. For two decades, they've merely survived, standing in endless lines for basic necessities, like a game of chance – eggs one day, rice the next."

Enedina bustling about the kitchen and occasionally joining the conversation, added humor, "I remember the egg frenzy! Hurry, grab those eggs before they disappear!" She enacted the scene, opening her beautiful opal blue eyes. "And did you hear about the brawl at the chicken distribution site?" The room erupted in laughter.

"That's sadly not uncommon," she continued.

"Absolutely, it made the headlines," Alfredo responded with a frown.

Gladys, leaning forward with wide-eyed amazement, contributed, "And soap! People here are buying a load of soap to send back to their families in Cuba. There's a shortage of everything, even basic hygiene items!"

Alfredo continued, his anger and disappointment palpable, "It's not only the destruction that Castro's government had done to industries, scarcity of food, medicines, essential goods, the adulteration of the soil, deterioration of buildings and homes for lack of building materials. A country that was so rich in sugar cane, tobacco, industry, and technology is now an impoverished country. But as if that is not enough, the system changed the personalities of a whole nation. They have transformed the nation's psyche. The system has fundamentally altered its people."

Gladys empathized, "Yes, and the obsession with material possessions has grown due to prolonged deprivation. Having expensive cars or designer clothes becomes a priority for some, overshadowing cultural pursuits. I understand," she continued, "The younger generation hasn't had the privilege of a solid education. I heard a priest during a Mass aired from Cuba on YouTube, 'Our kids need to have time to focus on their education instead of worrying about finding food. They need to grow up eating healthy food, playing carefree, and studying without worries.'"

"That's not happening in Cuba, and here we are already beholding the results of a whole generation negatively impacted by the communist regime." Alfredo continued with a heavy heart, "Communism worldwide not only destroys entire countries but its people as well, detrimentally impacting their spirit. Pre-1959, Cubans were enterprising, ambitious, and hard-working people. Now, their souls are worn down. Many have given up; others risk their lives leaving the island in pursuit of the torch of hope. But their spirits have been altered, no longer knowing how to fulfill their dreams. Their aspirations have been obscured by the fog of time. Their horizons have shriveled, but perhaps not irreversibly, and hopefully not forever. The hope is in the children. They hold the power to reverse the cycle. The forgotten spirit may rekindle when they discover the essence of the American Dream."

31

THE SWARMING CHOIR LADIES
Miami, Florida.
Summer 2000

Whenever the phone rang, Alfredo's habitual, gentle instructions to his granddaughters, Jenny and Jackie, were, "Tell them I'm not here."

In the summer of 2000, Alfredo relocated to Gladys' house, where he lived for the following year with her and her daughters, Jenny and Jackie. It was a period marked by the couple's mutual decision to bring an end to an era, signifying the conclusion of their marriage. Once the word spread through the church choir that Alfredo and Enedina had parted ways, the phone rang incessantly. "Hola. Is Alfredo home?"

The granddaughters found themselves at a loss, the calls were frequent and their reluctance to lie palpable, yet they dutifully adhered to their grandfather's wishes. He had been a member of a choir for years, and now, with his newfound availability, several of the older women in the choir had taken a keen interest in him.

"*¡Abuelo, te están cayendo como hormigas bravas*! - Grandpa, they are climbing on you like crazed ants!" Jenny playfully remarked.

Alfredo, unamused by the grandkid's jokes, would promptly deny the assertion, "No, they are only calling about

178

choir practices."

Jenny and Jackie would roll their eyes and exchange knowing glances, with Jackie quipping, "What a coincidence, right? Suddenly, there are so many practices."

"Abuelo, are you going to choir practice tonight?" Jenny asked on one occasion.

"I don't know. You are right. There seem to be too many practices," Grandpa replied despondently.

Following his separation, Alfredo found solace in the world of news, often choosing to stay in and watch TV. Occasionally, he would muster the energy to attend choir practice but would promptly return home.

On a warm Tuesday evening, upon his return home, Alfredo informed Gladys, "I don't think I'll be attending choir practices anymore."

"Why, Dad? You used to love it," Gladys inquired, puzzled by his statement.

"I love singing in the choir, but lately, it's become uncomfortable."

"Dad, what happened?" She dropped everything she was doing and studied him, trying to discern his emotions.

"I'll share that with you on another occasion. Right now, I only want to rest and watch the news."

She wondered what had caused this sudden change but decided not to press him with questions.

Several months later, while leisurely navigating the supermarket aisles with her shopping cart, Gladys ran into Teresa, one of the choir members. After exchanging greetings, Teresa inquired, "How is your dad? He's been missing choir practice and hasn't attended any recent gatherings. Is he ok?"

"He is a bit under the weather, feeling down, but otherwise ok," Gladys replied.

"We think something happened during the last practice he attended," Teresa revealed. "Mayra sat next to him, then Fran came over, claiming, 'That's my seat!' It led to an unpleasant confrontation. Mayra, being stubborn, refused to move, and Fran eventually left the room and never returned. It was clear they were fighting over him."

"But, Teresa, my dad is seventy-eight years old! Goodness, and they are fighting over him!" Gladys exclaimed in shock.

"It's not just Mayra and Fran. Carmen and Sylvia have shown interest in him, too. We all know he has no interest in anyone; his only interest is singing and reconciling with his wife. It's evident from his demeanor."

Alfredo and Enedina's divorce was finalized six months prior to their 50th wedding anniversary. Meanwhile, the choir ladies persisted with their best persuasive and flirtatious strategies, sometimes transforming into gladiators, viewing each other as obstacles in their desperate quest for the ultimate prize.

32

FABULOUS ME
Miami, Florida.
2000-2018

On a brisk September Saturday afternoon, Gladys eased her car out of the garage and into the driveway. Her eyes widened as she noticed her father, Alfredo, pulling in with his metallic green 1990s Malibu. It has been six months since Alfredo had moved into Gladys' home.

"Dad, are you ok?" Gladys inquired, stepping out of her car to greet him. He appeared different, exuding an air of happiness and vitality that made him seem younger, as if he'd been rejuvenated. His lively body language left a lasting impression on Gladys as he entered the house with an unusual smile on his face, a smile she hadn't seen since the fateful day of their parent's separation.

"*Si, encantado de la vida! -* Loving life!" He responded, his smile widening.

Gladys was taken aback by his unexpected response. *What's going on here?* She wondered, struck by his unexpected answer and unusual demeanor.

"Where were you?" she asked, attempting to sound discreet.

"Oh, I was at the airport. I took your Uncle Roman and Aunt Olguita to pick up a relative who flew in from Puerto Rico to visit them."

Uhm, she thought, still puzzled by the radiant aura surrounding him.

Following Roman's unfortunate leg amputation due to diabetes, Alfredo graciously extended his offer to chauffeur his brother-in-law and wife whenever transportation was required. Alfredo's willingness to drive them was not out of the ordinary. What stood out this one time was the radiant joy he exuded while doing so.

"Well, that's great, Dad. I'm heading to the supermarket, but I'll be right back," she replied, trying not to pry too much. *Umm, something different is happening here.*

She rushed to pick up a few things at the supermarket, hoping for a quick return that might yield some information. However, upon her return, Alfredo was engrossed in the television, and nothing was said.

The next day, early as usual, Gladys prepared her daughters for school and herself for work and left before Alfredo was up. At about 4:30 pm, on her return from work and picking up her daughters from school, she arrived home. Unloading the car, papers from work, kids' book bags, and lunch bags, she heard, "Mom, I'm hungry, can I have a snack before dinner?" As Gladys attempted to answer her daughter Jackie, they were all taken by the vision of the handsome, well-dressed, and perfumed grandfather.

"Abuelo, why are you so nicely dressed? Wow. You smell good. Where are you going?" Jenny asked.

"I'm going out! See you all later!" he replied, a smile accompanying a playful wink. "But Abuelo!"

And without any further explanation, he got in his car and left.

"What's wrong with him?" Jenny wondered.

"Uhm, I do not think there is anything wrong," Gladys replied.

Days turned into weeks, and Alfredo's outings continued until it reached the point that Alfredo was spending less time home and more time out.

Several weeks later, it was revealed that, coincidentally, on the day of the airport outing, a relative of Olguita, who also happened to be one of the church choir ladies, was also at the airport. It was there that Alfredo's avoidance of romance was suddenly reversed by Cupid's arrow. He had fallen head over heels for Mayra, a woman Alfredo described as "so beautiful" embodying the notion that love is blind, even though not everyone shared his perception of her appearance. Mayra, was a slightly heavy-set seventy-eight-year-old lady who took great pride in her appearance, always dressing well, standing straight, and wearing sandals with short heels. She ensured that her hair and nails were impeccably maintained and reveled in compliments about her looks. Mayra rejoiced in sharing stories of how she was constantly praised for her looks.

"Oh! How pretty you look today." People would say in response to her body language,

She possessed the special talent of portraying the image of: *Here comes fabulous me* and *I'm the last Coke in the desert.*

Some may fall for this projected image.

About a year later, Alfredo and Mayra got married, in part due to pressure from some very religious relatives who were worried about Alfredo living a sinful life in concubinage with this lady.

For a few years, they enjoyed a happy marriage, and

Alfredo found the happiness that he had lost years before. Though hesitant about the intrusion of this unexpected person in their lives, his family rejoiced in his newfound happiness.

"Alfredo is great!" Mayra would often declare with a mysterious smile that left others wondering.

But one hot and sunny afternoon in Miami, upon returning from the supermarket, Mayra screamed, "You are having an affair with the cashier lady at the supermarket!" Her face transformed, her eyes narrowed, and she unleashed a torrent of unfounded accusations, transforming her from a loving wife into a raging monster.

"You are crazy! Why would you say that?" Alfredo responded in shock. "With the cashier, of all people? At the supermarket?"

Overnight, Mayra's demeanor changed drastically for the worse. For several months she made their lives a living hell. Strangely, this shift occurred a few months after a significant water leak in their apartment, leading to mold infestation. They had to remove furniture and belongings, clean extensively, and use moisture removal equipment for weeks.

During a visit, Gladys encountered Mayra's son, Ronald, in the parking lot, the family medical doctor who had been treating his mother. "Hi Ronald, have you finally been able to diagnose your mom's illness?" Gladys asked. "We would like to know since it affects my dad's life and ours, too."

"She has a form of Alzheimer's that resembles schizophrenia." He explained. "It's a debilitating disease, and she'll deteriorate further until it takes her life."

Gladys was in shock. "Are you sure? Could it be related

to the mold she was exposed to for so long? I have looked-up some information and found that mold may cause similar mental problems."

"No, no, no, it's not related to mold. I wish I could tell you otherwise; but you and your sister will need to make arrangements for your dad. They're both in their 80s, we will probably need to take her somewhere for specialized care, and he shouldn't be alone."

Fortunately, the doctor's diagnosis proved to be incorrect, and the scientific research about mold turned out to be accurate. A few months later, with the moldy situation resolved, Mayra miraculously recovered, and their happy life resumed for several more years.

33

THE FOREVER-AWAITED DEATH OF FIDEL

Rockville, Maryland.
November 25ᵗʰ, 2016

"Fidel is Dead!" The startling news flashed on Gladys' cell phone at the stroke of midnight.

"No! This can't be real!" she replied in a frenzy, her room a whirlwind as she desperately scoured her phone for any confirmation of the news, "This cannot be happening!" Her mind was in turmoil. "Oh, my goodness! Is it really true? How did it happen? We all heard he was sick, but never believed anything the Cuban government said."

It was November 25, 2016, well past midnight when Gladys received the news, "I have to call my dad! Do you think he knows?" Without waiting for a response, she continued, "No, he would have called me if he knew. He doesn't know. I have to call him."

"No, you can't call him now; he's asleep, and at ninety-four, news like this might endanger his weak heart," replied Javier, Gladys' friend.

"But how can I *not* tell him! How can he *not* know? He's spent a lifetime waiting for this moment!" Gladys paced the room, torn about what to do, what to say, where to go.

"I'm going downstairs to watch the news on TV," she declared, rushing out of the room and heading for the basement. In the dimly lit basement, she fumbled to find the remote control, discovering four of them and pressing each one in turn, unsure which would work. The house lay silent; everyone else was asleep. It was Thanksgiving weekend in 2016, and Gladys found herself at Javier's relative's house in Rockville, Maryland, far from Miami, where her family eagerly awaited this momentous news.

Calm down Gladys, she thought. *First, figure out which remote turns on the TV. This one must be for the DVD. Let me check the brands and the labels.* Her anxiety drove her to hop from one remote control to the other. *This one says cable; this one has the same name as the TV unit. This must be the first one I need to use. I wish our hosts, Lauren or Kevin, were awake to help me with this. I can't get it right,* she muttered to herself in vexation.

Why isn't Javier excited about this? I wish he offered to help me with these confounded controls and this idiotic TV. She rushed back upstairs in search of help.

"Please, help me," she implored, grabbing Javier's shoulder. "I can't turn it on. There are too many controls, and I don't know which one it is. I have tried them all."

Despite Javier's Cuban heritage, he had spent the past forty-three years residing in the central United States, engrossed in his family and career. This prolonged distance from the Cuban situation had somewhat insulated him from its immediate impact. In stark contrast, Gladys, who had been living in Miami for a comparable number of years, found the news to be much more resonant and significant.

"Nothing will change," Javier replied.

"What do you mean? You don't understand because you haven't lived in Miami, where we've all spent our lives waiting for this moment."

"Still, Gladys, nothing will change in Cuba now. Fidel has been sick for too long, and the regime continues with his brother."

"But you don't understand what this means!" She retorted with the anger of being misunderstood, the frustration of being away at this important moment her family had longed for, along with their compatriots.

"We've waited all our lives for this moment, and when it happens, the world surrounding me responds: So, what?"

Gladys' eyes flashed with anxiety; her face contorted with distress. "Do you know how many people have died dreaming and hoping for this moment? Do you know how many lives were put on hold waiting for this?

Gladys tried to explain to Javier the meaning of this event for the people that she knew.

"Well, I need to turn on the TV, and I can't. Could you please, help me with that?" she pleaded.

Running downstairs for the second time, Gladys resumed her desperate attempts to decipher the TV's remote controls. Finally, she managed to tune into a news station. But to her dismay, there was nothing - no news about Castro's death. *If I were in Miami,* she thought, *I'm certain every local station would be covering this event.* It felt like an eternity as she kept searching for information.

Then, suddenly, she stumbled upon a broadcast, "Cuban leader Fidel Castro has passed away."

"That's it! Come on! Can't you provide a bit more

detail?" Gladys shouted at the TV in a fit of frustration. She couldn't fathom the newscaster's indifference to the most crucial news of her life. With a sense of apathy, he continued on to report some other irrelevant news, leaving Gladys baffled and exasperated.

Drained by her fruitless quest for information and overwhelmed with frustration, she retreated to her room, attempting to sleep, but of course, sleep eluded her all night long. She may have dozed off for an hour or two, only to wake up, check her phone for news, and repeat the cycle throughout the night.

She couldn't stop thinking, *How would Dad feel when he hears the news? I can't wait until it's morning and I can call him. Oh Lord, what am I doing here so far from Miami? If I were in Miami, I would be heading to Versailles. I'm sure people are already gathering there for the celebration.* All night long, her brain did not stop. *I may take a flight home tomorrow. It's the moment for the greatest celebration back home and I am missing the joy of sharing it with my people.*

Gladys knew exactly when her dad would wake up. At 7:05 am, she dialed his number, "Dad, have you heard the news!"

"I'm listening to it right now!" She heard the excitement in his voice, followed by the jubilant shout, "*Viva Cuba Libre!* - Long live free Cuba." With the phone to his ear, he continued listening to the news on the TV and then he said, "*Coño, por fin ese diablo se murió* - Damn, finally that devil died. Not even Satan wanted him in hell. How many of my friends, who are now dead, would have given everything they had in their lives for a taste of this moment!" His voice trembled with emotion.

His wife's enthusiastic voice is heard in the back, "Listen to what *The Miami Herald* says: 'Cuban exiles pour onto Miami streets to celebrate the end of Castro's deathful era.'"

"Gladys, the TV stations are going crazy reporting from Little Havana. If you could only see the faces of all these people, the joy, the tears of happiness. Listen to what some people are saying," Alfredo directed the phone toward the TV, so Gladys could hear the news reports.

"This is a celebration, but not a celebration of death, a beginning of liberty that we've been waiting for many years. The hope is that it opens up Cuba a little bit more," a Cuban-American man said.

All phones are ringing at the same time, my cell phone, the house phone, "Hello! ¡*Pilar, oiste*! - Pilar, did you hear the news?" Maria answered two different phones simultaneously.

"Alfredo, your sister Pilar and Roberto are on the phone! Ronald is on the other phone, *Mi hijo*, this is incredible! Finally! Yes, here is Alfredo on the other line talking to family in Puerto Rico!" Mayra exclaimed nervously, juggling two phones.

Gladys was left speechless, savoring the jubilation of her beloved dad and his wife. Alfredo with a phone in one hand and the TV remote in the other, simultaneously reached for the other phones that his wife was handing over to him.

"*¡Mi hermana como hemos esperado este momento!* - My sister, how long we've waited for this moment!" Gladys could feel the emotion pouring through the phone as Alfredo spoke to his 88-year-old sister, Pilar, and her husband, Roberto, the brother-in-law who tried to convince Alfredo fifty-six years ago that Castro was a communist and an assassin. In that somber September 1960 phone conversation, Alfredo had finally acknowledged that Roberto had been right all along. Due to this *traitor*, which most Cubans had supported in the revolution, he and his family had been forced to abandon their country, leaving behind their possessions and dreams.

"What have you heard in Puerto Rico? Are they celebrating?" Alfredo inquired.

"We just woke up, heard the news, and Roberto said, 'Miami must be going crazy, let's call Alfredo!'" Pilar replied with eagerness.

Alfredo continued, "Listen to what they are saying on TV, 'The scene across Miami-Dade County, the cradle of the Cuban exile community, is one of pure, raw emotion. This time, after decades of false alarms, Castro's death is finally real.'" Alfredo stopped, savoring the moment.

"Listen to what this young man said on TV this morning at 2:00 am, 'I wish my dad were here to see this,'" Alfredo explained. "A 27-year-old guy who was crying while being interviewed in the midst of the early morning celebration."

"Dad, this is the sentiment of many young people who watched their parents suffer through years of exile, only to pass away waiting for this moment that never arrived for them," Gladys reflected. "These people are experiencing this moment with a mixture of happiness and sadness in their hearts, thinking, *If only our parents, our beloved elders, could have witnessed the joy of their lifetimes by experiencing this long-awaited historical moment.*"

"Dad, listen to what I'm reading on my phone from Twitter," she added enthusiastically. "In Little Havana, Miami, the crowd celebrating Fidel Castro's death is singing

La Bayamesa, the Cuban national anthem. It's quite a moment!"

"Dad, I'm booking a flight. I have to celebrate this moment with you." Gladys said to her dad, tears welling up in her eyes.

"No Gladys, don't come," he replied. "I know we've all waited a lifetime for this moment, but you see, it's really too late. We all want to believe that change will come, but the truth is, that nothing will change, the dream was snatched away from us forever. The most awaited moment of our lives has finally arrived!" he said, raising his arms in a victorious gesture before letting them fall again, "But you know what? This moment arrived too late."

34

THE LONG-AWAITED REUNION

Miami, Florida.
October 2018

On a clear and sun-drenched October afternoon in Miami, the atmosphere exuded a refreshing crispness, casting a luminous aura upon the vibrant cityscape. Alfredo, who, because of poor health conditions, had been living with his daughter Mary and her husband for the last three months, was celebrating his 96th birthday.

Over the past several years, his family had always eagerly organized birthday celebrations for him. They understood that time was running out, and every moment with him and his family was precious.

"Mary, what can we do this year to celebrate Dad's birthday?" Gladys asked her sister. Each year, they would plan an outing with the family, with a preference for Spanish restaurants featuring live music. Alfredo, who had a beautiful voice, would often sing along. His voice was always noticed, and he was frequently encouraged to join in, *"Alfredo, vamos, canta La Paloma* - Alfredo, come, sing La Paloma."

La Paloma was composed and written by the Spanish composer from the Basque region Sebastián Iradier in the 1850s. It was certainly the most-recorded Spanish song. This song was Alfredo's favorite and frequently requested by his

193

family and friends.

However, this year was different. Alfredo could no longer eat regular food due to his PEG (Percutaneous Endoscopic Gastrostomy) procedure, which had been necessary because of difficulty swallowing. Despite his neuropathy, poor vision, and inability to eat, he remained cheerful, alert and engaged in conversations with anyone who visited him.

"How can we celebrate his birthday if he can't leave the house and can't even eat?" Mary wondered.

"Well, I'm coming over to spend time with him for his birthday," Gladys replied.

"Well, we've decided to have a small gathering with just the immediate family," Mary informed her sister during a phone call later that evening.

Five years earlier, Gladys had noticed that their mom, Enedina, was no longer able to live independently. She had moved Enedina into her own beautiful home, where she had raised her two daughters.

Enedina hadn't laid eyes on Alfredo in more than 15 years since their separation and divorce. She had unequivocally conveyed, both in words and deeds, that she had no desire whatsoever to see him again.

However, one of the benefits of dementia is that deep-seated emotions, even hatred, may be forgotten.

"It's been over fifteen years, and I'm tired of this family separation. I think I'm bringing Mom to Dad's birthday gathering." Gladys said aloud. She had made up her mind and did not care what anyone thought. *I won't tell anyone. They'll think I've lost my mind. But I really don't care. We don't have many more family reunions left, so I'm doing this.*

She thought as she made her bed on that crisp, beautiful October morning.

"Mom let's get dressed. We are going to a birthday party." Gladys told her mother.

"Whose birthday party?" Enedina inquired.

"You will see! It's a surprise!" Gladys responded with a smile. "Let's find some beautiful clothes for you to wear. I want you to look very pretty today."

Even at the age of 93, Enedina's stunning azure eyes continued to earn compliments. Gladys could sense a unique happiness within her as she prepared to reunite her parents after almost 15 years of separation.

Gladys recalled all those years when she had to plan two Thanksgiving gatherings, one for her mother and one for father. Her daughters would assist her by attending both parties, sometimes one right after the other. A year after her parents' divorce, Gladys had organized an early Thanksgiving lunch for her mom on her terrace by the pool, on a perfect breezy and clear day for an outdoor gathering. The laughter and memories flowed amidst plants, flowers, and the hanging bougainvillea under the trellis in Gladys' backyard.

"There is a guy at the elderly center who plays guitar, and he sang a song about my blue eyes in front of everyone," Enedina had shared during that delightful conversation.

"Oh no! Abuela. He likes you!" Jenny responded among the laughter of the group. "Do you like him?"

"No way! He is an old man! I'm not going to give up my freedom to wash an old man's underwear," Enedina replied evoking everyone's smile.

"Abuela, now men wash their own underwear! You're

thinking we're still in Spain in the nineteen-forties!" The laughter continued amidst the breeze of that beautiful afternoon.

After a three-hour lunch, Gladys made a signal to her daughters that it was time to wrap up the gathering. They all helped to clean up.

"Goodbye, Abuelita! We're all leaving now to attend a Thanksgiving party at Jenny's boyfriend's house. And mom is coming with us!"

The girls fabricated this story because Enedina had no intention of leaving anytime soon. However, Alfredo was already parked around the corner, seated inside his car, patiently waiting his turn. The girls were helping with the situation because they knew Grandpa was waiting for her to leave. Alfredo didn't have any reservations about sharing the same space with her, but it was Enedina who firmly refused to participate in any event where he would be present. No one in the family dared to bring up the topic.

"She is like Old Faithful!" Gladys would jest with family when discussing the possibility of reuniting them. "She could be perfectly calmed, like the Old Faithful geyser in Yellowstone, and suddenly, without any warning, Bam! An explosion! Like the enormous, magnificent eruption of the geyser," she explained. "Then, just as suddenly, it would stop, and you wouldn't even suspect anything had happened."

"That's her!" Family members would reply, almost singing and with a smile on their faces. They understood that any little thing could trigger Enedina's emotions, so they played along, keeping the couple apart for more than fifteen years.

On October 21, 2018, Gladys drove Enedina to her other daughter's house. Ubaldo, Mary's husband, opened the door, and upon seeing Enedina, he took a step back, widened his eyes, and let out a startled laugh. Turning to the side to prevent Enedina from hearing him, he exclaimed, "Oh my God, why did you bring her? Mary is going to have a heart attack."

Then Mary came to the door and said to Gladys, "Are you crazy?" Then, rapidly turning toward her mother, trying to conceal her panic, she said, "Hi, Mom." Her face was a mix of panic, horror, and bewilderment.

"We only have a few years left to live, and I really want to do this. Let's do it!" Gladys replied as she helped Enedina up the entrance steps. Mary and Ubaldo remained by the door, petrified, with panic-stricken expressions as mother and daughter made their way into the house.

Alfredo, who had anticipated the arrival of other family members, initially smiled but then experienced a whirlwind of emotions as he laid eyes on Enedina. His eyes sparkled with a blend of panic, surprise, and overwhelming joy. Enedina had always been the love of his life, and he hadn't seen her in over fifteen years. Emotions flooded his senses.

Gladys gently asked, "Mom, do you remember this person?" As Enedina navigated her dementia, she had become adept at concealing whether she remembered or not. Her family couldn't discern the truth because she had a way of acting as though she did. Alfredo longed to embrace her but was uncertain if he should. The rest of the family in the room stood in shock. They were well aware of the situation but had never expected this moment to materialize. Everyone's eyes were wide open, and their mouths were ready to drop. No one could take their eyes off the couple. Tailleen, one of the granddaughters, pulled out her cell phone and began recording the expressions on both faces.

Gladys guided her mom to a chair beside Alfredo. The entire family, including daughters, grandchildren, great-grandchildren, and in-laws, gathered around, eager to witness the unfolding drama.

Figure 17 - Alfredo and Enedina surrounded by family, October 21, 2018.

"Abuela, do you know who he is?" Tailleen asked. Enedina leaned her head forward, seemingly affirming the question. The room's collective eyes widened.

"Do you remember his name?" Tailleen persisted. Enedina acted as if she knew but chose not to respond. She had perfected the act of convincing others that her mind remained sharp.

"Abuela, do you remember that you were married to him?" Tailleen asked, and Enedina continued to indicate affirmatively with her movements. As the initial surprise subsided and Mary and the others realized that Old Faithful, as they affectionately refer to her in certain occasions, was not acting out today, the conversation resumed. Cameras were out in full force, videotaping and capturing this historic moment, and a deluge of questions followed.

"Abuelo, why don't you tell Abuela some stories about Santiago de Cuba and when you both met?" Alfredo, at the age of 96, possessed a memory as sharp as an elephant and began recounting their most cherished memories. He recalled every significant date and intricate detail from his life as he embarked on recounting their most cherished memories.

"I first crossed paths with you through your brother, Gallego, during our time as fellow students at the Commerce School of Santiago de Cuba. One evening, I stopped by your house to pick up a book, and there you were!" Alfredo paused to catch his breath, his eyes moist with tears. "I was mesmerized by your gorgeous blue eyes," he confessed.

Enedina replied, "Oh, that must have been my sister. You must be thinking about her. She was prettier than me."

"No, it was not your sister. We've had this conversation before. It was you!" Alfredo stopped to scrutinize her expression before continuing. "There was a large window in the living room that faced the street, and right across was the Church of Santa Lucia. Remember?" He kept pausing, studying her face for any hints of memories. "Your dad was the priest's best friend, and they used to gather in the evenings at your house to enjoy the church wine. They claimed it was the best wine in town." Laughter filled the room as the attentive audience closely listened to these vivid memories.

"A few days later at school, I told your brother, 'I really

like your sister! Do you think I have a chance with her?" Alfredo continued cautiously, always attentive to her reactions. "But your brother responded, Are you out of your mind? She's strong-willed with a fiery temper! Be careful what you are getting into."

"Every day," Alfredo continued, "I'd causally appeared in one of the side streets near your school just to catch a glimpse of you. Remember? And I used to say, 'Oh, what a coincidence! I happened to be in the neighborhood for work. May I walk you home?'"

"Abuela, do you remember?" Sebastian, one of the great-grandkids, asked. Enedina nodded affirmatively, but the audience couldn't ascertain whether she genuinely remembered or was skillfully feigning it.

"Eight months later, we were getting married!"

"No! Just eight months!" one of the grandkids exclaimed while the others laughed.

"Abuelo, why so fast?" asked one of the kids.

This time, Enedina responded, astounding the audience, "It was because of my sister; she wouldn't leave us alone. She was our chaperone, and she drove us crazy. We had to get rid of her!" The revelation of these memories of the dementia patient left everyone in shock. It was a testament of the unpredictable nature of the disease.

On this magical October afternoon, Alfredo mesmerized his family with the intricate details of his memories. No one wanted the afternoon to end.

"Gladys, you have to bring me here more often so this man can share more of these stories with me," Enedina said to her daughter. Her desire for more time with him, after avoiding him for all those years, stunned the witnesses of this remarkable afternoon.

Alfredo cherished every single moment and didn't want the afternoon to end. The family longed to freeze this blissful moment in time.

As Gladys rose to assist her mom to the car, she could sense that her dad's eyes were pleading, "Please, don't take her away!" He voiced only one request, "Promise me you'll bring her back soon."

Then Tailleen turned to Enedina and asked, "Abuela, would you marry him again?" Everyone, except Enedina, froze.

Enedina, her gaze fixed on her granddaughter, paused for a moment. Then, with conviction and a radiant smile, she responded,

"Yes, why not?"

35

WINGS OF FREEDOM

Miami, Florida.
January 12, 2019

"I think he is dead." The dreadful phone call shattered the silence around 6:00 am.

"What do you mean?" Gladys responded with confusion, when she abruptly received the most terrible, unexpected news, in the middle of her sleep. She leaped out of bed, clutching her cell phone tightly.

"What happened?" she asked, alarmed at the shocking revelation.

"He's not waking up. I've called 911, and they're on their way," Mary replied.

"I'm on my way!" Gladys declared, still gripping the phone. She hastily threw on jeans and a blouse, hurriedly brushed her teeth, and dashed out the door.

The somber expressions on the faces of the rescue squad members delivered the answer she dreaded.

"Sorry, ma'am." they offered with deep sympathy before leaving.

"He died peacefully in his sleep," the words hung heavily in the air as she approached his bed. "Gladys, he was ninety-six. It was time for him to rest."

His countenance appeared serene, radiating an unusual kind of tranquility and even a hint of joy, as if he had glimpsed the face of God.

Gladys took a seat beside him, gently holding his hand, and whispered, "We love you, Dad. Thank you for all you gave us. Thank you for all your struggles to give us a better life. Thank you for your example of life. Thank you for your love. Now, you can finally return. Now you have the wings to fly back to the country that you loved and missed so much. You've done far more for us and so many others than you ever had to. Now, you may fly away in peace."

Gladys noticed a faint twitch on his face, followed by the tranquility of a gentle breeze as though a bird was gliding through the air, carried by the passing wind. *He's flying.* She could feel it through the lifeless touch of his hand. The words of Leo Tolstoy echoed in her mind as she adapted them to her situation. It *was many, many years ago, in a kingdom by the sea, that a man there lived whom you may know by the name of Alfredo. And this man he lived with no other thought than to love, serve, and eventually return to his adored homeland.*

She just knew—*He's back. He is in the hands of God. He has returned to the place where he belongs.*

For all those like Alfredo, who has passed away in exile, may God grant you the wings to finally return to your homeland.

~~~

Memories, though fading with time, persist within the labyrinths of Enedina's dementia-riddled mind. And suddenly, when least expected, they surface.

"Did he arrive?"

"Who, Mom?"

"That man that sleeps here in this bed."
~~~

"Who, Mom?"

Then, gazing into the distance, a puzzled expression on her face, she says,

"Alfredo, of course!"

Figure 18- Enedina and Alfredo, rekindling the love of youth.

OUR FAMILY

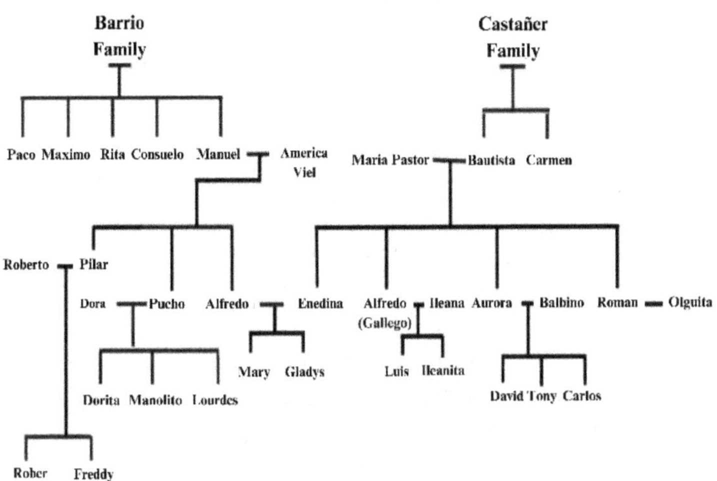

OTHER CHARACTERS IN ALPHABETICAL ORDER

This story is based on real facts. However, any resemblance to other locales or circumstances or any persons, living or deceased, is entirely coincidental. Below is a list of characters and their relationships among them. Some names have been changed to protect their identities.

Alejo Cabrera	Alfredo and Roman's business partner.
Antonio	Enedina's cousin.
Celia	Olguita's sister.
Father Arteta	Pastor of the Santa Lucia Catholic Church parish who also was Bautista's friend. Enedina and Alfredo were married by the hands of this priest.
Jacoba	Lady who raised Manuel Barrio in Spain.

Javier	Gladys' friend.
Lucia	Enedina's cousin.
Mayra	Alfredo's second wife.
Mariano	A poor malnourished young boy who ran errands for money in Santiago de Cuba.
Mateo	Bautista's youth friend in Spain.
Miguel Pons	Foreman of the Castañer's coffee plantation.
Nora	Enedina and Alfredo's housekeeper in Cuba.
Omero	Family gardener and former Cuban political ex-prisoner.
Pascual	Bautista's cousin.
Pepe and Nina	Tía Carmen's children.
Ronald	Mayra's sons.
Rosita	Enedina's friend from school.

March 15, 1964

Queridos mami y papi,

Estoy echándoles mucho de menos, mis tíos me dan mucho cariño, pero no es igual sin ustedes.

Vengan pronto, hacemos lo posible para que salgan, les echo mucho de menos. Ponce es MUY caluroso y mi cuarto no tiene aire, gracias mi tio me compro un "abanico" en Cuba les dicen "VENTILADOR eléctrico" y con eso las paso mas o menos, tambien hay mucho mosquito en Ponce, (la casa no tiene 'tela metalica' en Ponce le dicen SCREEN).

Como me prometiste, cuando lleguen me compran mi caballito, como el que teníamos en CIUDAMAR, le echo mucho de menos. Así como Silva, ¿verdad? Ustedes saben que su nombre era Silver que quiere decir plata. Ahora que estoy aprendiendo ingles me di cuenta que no era Silva de silvar.

En la escuela todo bien, tengo muchos amigos nuevos y me meterán en los BOY SCOUTS. Grupo como los pioneritos en Cuba, pero sin adoctrinarme, ni darme clases de comunismo, como querían hacerme en Cuba.

Rober

ACKNOWLEDGMENTS

Often in life, the value of the efforts of our ancestors goes unnoticed and diminishes with time. One day, when I finally took a moment to reflect, these thoughts and memories coalesced in me. That day, I realized that a deeper understanding of the actions of our ancestors is what carved the individuals we are today. This book is the result of the love and struggles of three generations of my family, which suddenly exploded in my mind and gave birth to this story.

On that note, I would like to start by acknowledging all my ancestors, whether named or not, whose DNA traces are imbued in me and my descendants, the qualities that make us who we are today.

I hope the following words will serve to acknowledge and thank those who have played an invaluable role in bringing my story to light.

My dear cousin, Rober Bory, who I consider the brother I never had, generously shared the events and deep feelings of his exile story, which is included in the chapter, *Letters from Rober*.

Omero, our family gardener and once political prisoner of the Castro regime, offered his harrowing account of the inhumane conditions and abuses he endured in Cuban jails and prison camps. His words to me were, "I want the world to hear these stories and the horror stories of all those like me who suffered torture at the hands of the Cuban communist government."

My dear aunt Aurora Castañer, who recently passed at the age of 98, with a perfect, clear mind and memory, and related the stories of our family during the Spanish Civil War in the 1930s.

My mother, Enedina Castañer, who is almost 100 years old, vividly remembers childhood stories of her, her siblings, and her parents. The memories of her teenage and later years are clouded by dementia. But she clearly remembers the happy years as a little girl on the coffee plantation in Cuba. She will tell, over and over, the stories of her father calling the coffee workers to cover the picked coffee grains when rain was approaching. The stories of their donkey with whom they played as kids have fascinated all those blessed with hearing her animated tales.

My aunt Pilar Barrio, also in her 90s but with an amazing memory, patiently related their childhood and ancestors' stories to me. These stories are spread throughout the book and in the chapter: *Papá, Papá, Mate a Mariano.*

My dear father, Alfredo Barrio, told me the stories of his immigrant ancestors. He shared the story of his birth in a barn and his memories of his kindergarten teacher, who he remembered even at the age of 96. He spoke of his childhood, his romance with my mother, and the painful stories of our family's exile and the multiple restarts of his life. He narrated many of these stories just a few months before he passed away at the age of 96. None of the family members gathered around him on the day of his last birthday will forget his gentle, loving words to my mother, his wife of fifty years.

Jesus, my fiancé, has believed in me and encouraged me from the start of this new path as a writer.

I am also deeply thankful to my first editor, Deborah De Nicola, who without her initial corrections, enhancements, suggestions, encouragement, and guidance in interweaving the diverse stories, this book might not have come to fruition. Her invaluable assistance in character development significantly contributed to the final product.

However, the utmost gratitude goes to Susana Mueller, the editor who not only enhanced this book with her editorial comments but also meticulously structured it, collaborated on the visuals, and facilitated its transformation into a polished final edition. Her remarkable patience with me deserves special recognition.

My dear writing group has been an ongoing source of inspiration and encouragement. Sharon Wylie, our language arts teacher, reminded me of the grammatical rules I had long forgotten. Regine Rayevsky Fisher set a continuous example of great writing and was always a source of inspiration. Rachel Robbins's weekly stories of self-improvement and resiliency were motivating. Ernie Boudet's descriptions of nature helped me understand the importance of visual-surroundings in a story. My dear Judy Colina, our great hostess who, with her delightful family stories, put smiles on our faces every week. You kept our group together and always encouraged us to keep writing. David Lapham, you have kindly and patiently criticized my writings while continuously providing editorial comments and suggesting better ways of carving my thoughts. Your input has greatly influenced and improved my stories.

I extend my heartfelt gratitude to my Non-fiction Critique group, guided by Peter Lynk, whose invaluable feedback and corrections have significantly enhanced my writing. Special thanks to Scott Scovel, Brian Shaer, and other temporary participants for their contributions to the group.

And finally, my two daughters and five grandkids were the sparking light in the production of this project. Jenny and Jackie, "Your support and motivation carried me through to the end of this book. Thank you!"

EPILOGUE

We never heard anyone praising Antonio for his act of courage. Maybe my mother's siblings were too young to fully understand his bravery. Perhaps the memories were too painful to remember.

What an act of kindness! How much we owe our cousin, Antonio! At this time, no one knows if he survived the war or how much he suffered. We only know that his bravery and kindness spared our family from untold anguish.

We don't know how to thank Antonio for sparing our family from the inevitable suffering we, thank God, never knew and how his act of kindness ensured our descendance. We will be forever grateful to this brave man and those like him. Because of their selfless acts, we are all here today.

Many years later, at the age of 97, Aurora's eyes glistened, remembering Antonio.

Mas de las Matas sustained a great deal of damage during the coalition of the military forces; we also know that hundreds were killed, and women were savagely raped. Picasso's masterpiece, *Guernica,* provides a glimpse of what my maternal family lived through during those days and nights.

~~~

I would like to highlight here the work of a person who has been so many times underestimated. Jimmy Carter, the 39th President of the United States (1977-1981), was actively involved in promoting human rights around the world both during and after his presidency. One notable instance was his efforts to secure the release of political prisoners in Cuba.
~~~

In 2002, Carter visited Cuba, becoming the first former U.S. president to do so since the Cuban Revolution in 1959. During his visit, Carter met with then-President Fidel Castro and engaged in discussions about human rights and political prisoners in Cuba. Carter's visit aimed to foster better relations between the United States and Cuba while addressing concerns about political freedoms.

While in Cuba, Carter advocated for the release of several political prisoners. He raised awareness about their cases and urged the Cuban government to consider their release as a gesture of goodwill. Although his visit did not result in the immediate release of all prisoners, it contributed to a dialogue on human rights issues and ultimately resulted in the release of hundreds of Cuban prisoners.

Carter's commitment to human rights extended beyond Cuba, as he was involved in many international efforts to promote democracy, monitor elections, and address humanitarian issues. His post-presidential work reflects a dedication to advancing the cause of human rights and fostering global understanding.

Omero and countless others find it challenging to articulate their profound gratitude toward Jimmy Carter. Their lives, along with those of their families, have been enriched by the freedom and prosperity afforded to them through Carter's tireless work and dedication.

Gladys Barrio was born in Cuba, raised in Puerto Rico, and relocated to Miami, FL., where she presently lives. Gladys was always fascinated by literature, mathematics, and science. She completed a bachelor's in science degree from the University of Puerto Rico, followed by a master's program at Ohio State University, and ultimately was awarded a Ph.D. in Physical Chemistry from the University of Miami, Coral Gables, Florida. She conducted scientific research in various fields, including Thermodynamics and Groundwater Contamination, about which she produced over twenty-five scientific publications and numerous presentations. Later in her life, she became the High School District Executive Director and the Science Supervisor for the Miami-Dade County Public Schools, the fourth largest district in the Nation.

As an adjunct professor, she taught chemistry and Methods of Teaching Science at Florida International University, Miami-Dade College, and the University of Miami. Dr. Barrio has two accomplished daughters and five beautiful grandkids who are the inspiration for many of her stories. She always dreamed of writing the saga of her parents, including her mom's epic during the Spanish Civil War of 1936, followed by the Cuban exile of the 1960s when they had to forsake family and possessions in search of freedom and a better life.

ENDNOTES

1 See Appendix A: Family Tree and Other Characters

2 O'Grady, Mary Anastasia (30 December 2005). "Counting Castro's Victims". *Wall Street Journal*.

3 "Cuba's repressive machinery". Human Rights Watch. 1999.

4 Kern Alexander & Jon Mills, Resolving Property Claims in a Post-Socialist Cuba, 27 LAW & POL'Y INT'L BUS. 137, 178-179 (1995).

5 https://blogs.icrc.org/cross-files/the-icrc-and-the-evacuation-of-children-during-the-spanish-civil-war/

6 Bautista Castañer and Maria, his wife, will later have four kids including Enedina their younger daughter.

7 *Pardo Sanz, Rosa María (1995). "Antifascismo en América Latina: España, Cuba y Estados Unidos durante la Segunda Guerra Mundial". Estudios Interdisciplinares de América Latina y el Caribe (in Spanish).*

8 https://www.ascecuba.org/asce_proceedings/land-use-in-cuba-before-and-after-the-revolution-economic-and-environmental-implications/ - Castro's regime was mishandling Cuba's agriculture and didn't rotate crops causing a downshift in harvest output.

9 https://en.wikipedia.org/wiki/1924_Cuba_hurricane

10 https://www.sciencedirect.com/science/article/abs/pii/S0264999314003587#:~:text=In%20the%20decade%20of%20the,the%20Great%20Depression%20in%20Spain.

11 https://www.loc.gov/collections/stars-and-stripes/articles-and-essays/a-world-at-war/timeline-1914-1921/

12 https://www.theguardian.com/travel/2006/nov/17/travelnews

13 https://www.iwm.org.uk/history/voices-of-the-first-world-war-the-submarine-war

14 https://sanctuaries.noaa.gov/news/may18/world-war-i-on-the-homefront.html#:~:text=By%20the%20end%20of%20World,200%20American%20ships%20in%20total.

15 https://cnrse.cnic.navy.mil/Installations/NS-Guantanamo-Bay/About/History/

16 https://avalon.law.yale.edu/20th_century/dip_cuba002.asp

17 Ameringer, Charles. *The Cuban Democratic Experience: The Auténtico Years, 1944–1952*. Gainesville: University Press of Florida

(2000) p. 189 ISBN 0-8130-2667-9

[18] https://www.jstor.org/stable/41945906

[19] https://thecatholicnewsarchive.org/?a=d&d=cst19611027-01.2.8

[20] https://www.jfklibrary.org/learn/about-jfk/jfk-in-history/the-bay-of-pigs

[21] https://www.britannica.com/event/Cuban-missile-crisis

[22] *"Testimonios - Colchones de dinamita y TNT para prisioneros"* (in Spanish). Archived from *the original* on June 16, 2011. Retrieved November 21, 2010.

[23] https://www.dailymail.co.uk/news/article-7238953/How-Castro-rigged-Cuban-prison-five-tons-explosives-three-undercover-CIA-defused-it.html.

[24] https://en.wikipedia.org/wiki/Conscription_in_Cuba#:~:text=Cuban%20conscription%20until%201991,-Cuban%20nationals%20were&text=Under%20this%20structure%2C%20it%20was,was%20established%20in%20November%201963.

[25] https://www.reddit.com/r/PropagandaPosters/comments/ojedb8/cuban_obligatory_military_service_3_years_of/

[26] https://www.cia.gov/readingroom/docs/CIA-RDP80T00942A000900030001-2.pdf

[27] https://www.washingtonpost.com/wp-srv/inatl/longterm/cuba/holguin_province.htm

[28] https://www.discoverpuertorico.com/article/plan-trip-along-la-ruta-panoramica

[29] These letters convey authentic experiences through the perspective of my cousin Robertico during ages ten through thirteen. To ensure clarity for the readers, the contents have undergone both translation and grammatical editing.

[30] https://www.npr.org/2011/11/19/142534943/pedro-pan-childrens-life-altering-flight-from-cuba